The Ultimate
Polish Cookbook

Master 111 Traditional Dishes From Poland

Slavka Bodic

Imprint: Independently published
Please sign up for free recipes
www.balkanfood.org

Introduction

Poland is one of the European countries, like Italy and France, where people crave comfort food. Polish history is well-known, but it looks like their cuisine has not been discovered yet. Sometimes Poland is also called the country of pierogi (dumplings) and potatoes, but their cuisine has much more to offer.

Polish food takes us back to the history of the country, its location, and its relations with the other states. These relations had a great impact on the shape of its cuisine. The Polish food was quite calorific and spicy in the middle ages, as they were made out of meat, fruits, spices, wheat, honey, and herbs. In this cookbook we present recipes that are normally eaten by local people. Usually these recipes were passed down from generation to generation, and many of them were perfected thanks to local chefs.

Polish cuisine is the combination of East and West, evolved through centuries, which makes local dishes unique. You can find the same recipes throughout Poland, but with different spices and tastes.

Table of Contents

Why Polish cuisine?

One of the outstanding characteristics of Polish food is that it is not great for your diet. You will certainly find the Polish cuisine on the top of the wish-lists of people who love and enjoy comfort food. Yes, it may not be of the healthiest food for those conscious of their diets or their weight, but you cannot deny that it tastes heavenly delicious. No one can deny the rich taste of Polish cuisine, but people also love it for the following characteristics as well.

- Polish food is served in big portions.
- Polish cuisine mostly consists of dishes which include vegetables, grains, mushrooms, and meat.
- In Polish cuisine, there is always an extra serving of sauce, butter and sour cream added to almost every served meal.
- Polish cuisine has mastered the unique art of blending two unlikely ingredients in the most delicious way possible.
- Mostly fried or stewed ingredients are used in the Polish dishes so you can sense a deep and heavenly delicious taste in their meals.

During the middle ages, herbs, wheat, meat, fruits, and spices were the main components of Polish meals. Every ingredient they used was local, and they grew or produced it on their own soil. At those times, Polish food was caloric, and they liked to eat spicy food. Also, Polish people enjoyed a lot of local beer and used their hands instead of utensils.

The essence of Polish foods is linked to the location of the country and its relationship with its neighbors as well. At that time, there was a very popular tradition of hunting throughout the region, and it was famous in

Poland as well. Polish people love and respect local wild mushrooms and forest fruits. It is also one of the reasons that until now, Polish people often organize family trips to local forests in their spare time.

The meat, fish, and vegetables at that time were preserved with salt, and they used the sun drying process as well. Polish people also adopted the fermentation and pickling processes a long time ago.

At the time of partition, the merging of countries and regions affected the Polish cuisine. This is how, in the end, it can be said that Polish food is the product of many cooking traditions reflected by the diversity of its peoples.

Food lovers know that Polish people are completely obsessed with pickling their cucumbers and cabbage with perfection. People buy these vegetables in bulk when they are in season and then try to perfect their picking techniques.

Sauerkraut is shredded and pickled cabbage, which is a Polish specialty. Sauerkraut is considered as spoiled food in some countries, But Polish people disagree with this theory. They rather enjoy a range of sour delicacies. Speaking of which, sauerkraut is a common ingredient of the many traditional Polish dishes.

Apart from pickled cabbage, pickled cucumbers are also served at major gatherings. Pickled cucumbers are always served at any party or family dinner. Pickled cucumbers and Bigos (hunter's stew) are very famous appetizers served with chilled vodka. You can even witness this tradition in pubs where they serve drinks with appetizers

The list of Polish gems isn't limited to just the pickled cucumbers and cabbage. It is much bigger than that. Many dishes are considered as the crown holder in the kingdom of Polish cuisine. Most of the dishes are passed from generation-to-generation. However, many of the dishes have been perfected at the royal courts. The culinary experts perfected these dishes there. Most of the famous dishes are enjoyed by the common people, and they have now become part of the folk tradition of Poland. There are many dishes that you must try, but my top ten are:

- ***Pierogi*** (Polish dumplings)
- ***Gołąbki*** (cabbage roll)
- ***Łazanki z kapustą i grzybami***
- ***Bigos*** (Hunter's stew)
- ***Kotlet schabowy*** (breaded pork cutlet)
- ***Rosół*** (broth/ chicken soup)
- ***Polskie naleśniki*** (Polish pancakes)
- ***Śledź w oleju z cebulą*** (Herring in oil with onion)
- ***Gulasz*** (Goulash)
- ***Polish croissant cookies***

About Poland

Poland is an important part of the European continent. This ninth largest country is surrounded by the forests from the northwestern parts of Europe, by seas of the Atlantic Ocean and by the fertile planes of the European and Asian frontiers. Don't forget the lakes; the largest lake districts are here in Poland. If you like to hike, then you will enjoy your summers because there are about 2000 lakes, including Sniardwy, which is about 13.7 miles long and 8.3 miles wide (and is the largest in Poland).

Poland is an all in one weather country as there are 3 types of conditions of weather which influence the climate of the country. The oceanic air blows from the west, the cold air from the Scandinavian countries or Russia, and the warmer air from the south. In winter, the weather gets colder and crisp due to the polar air and, in the mid-summer, the weather becomes warmer and dry due to the subtropical air; but in the late summer and autumn, this air brings pleasant days for its people.

The variety of ethnic communities was the reason for Poland's popularity before World War II. Apart from the ethnic Polish community, Ukrainians, Jews and Belarusians were the largest ones. These people were dispersed in different areas of the country, and the war was fatal for the population and the ethnic communities in Poland. At the moment Poland has around 38 million inhabitants.

Before World War 2, this country was known for agriculture but also mining. However, during the communist rule, Poland developed an industrial sector for running the state economy. From the mid of 1970s, the country's economic growth slowed down, and then in the 1980s hyperinflation ruined the economic structure of the country. This continued until the 1990s when the scale of inflation began to fall. In 2000 the inflation rate fell to 10% from 250% in 1990. Ups and downs were prevalent until 2014 when the economy of the country started stabilizing. Poland has been a member of the European Union since 2004, and that was the key contributor to the economic stability and growth

BREAKFAST

Egg Scramble With Sausage

Preparation time: 12 minutes
Cooking time: 30 minutes
Nutrition Facts (per serving): 344 Calories (Fat 24g, Protein 18g, Fiber 3g)

Ingredients (4 servings)
6 ounces smoked sausage, sliced 1/4-inch thick
1/2 medium onion, chopped
2 medium potatoes, peeled, cut into 1/2-inch cubes
2 tablespoons unsalted butter
1/2 medium green pepper, seeded, chopped
1 1/2 cups of sliced mushrooms
6 large eggs
Salt and pepper
1/4 cup of whole milk

Preparation
Place the potatoes and 2 teaspoons salt in a large, deep skillet and cover with 1-inch cold water. Bring to a boil and cook for 7-9 minutes or until potatoes are just tender. Drain and wipe the skillet clean.

Melt butter in the same skillet over medium-high heat. Add the sausage. Cook, stirring occasionally for 3-4 minutes or until browned on both sides. Remove from the skillet with a slotted spoon and place in a bowl. Add the vegetables to the pan; season with salt and pepper. Cook over medium heat, stirring occasionally, for 7-9 minutes or until the mushrooms are browned and the vegetables are tender.

Beat the eggs with milk in a bowl. Season with salt and pepper. Add sausage and potatoes to vegetables in a skillet and stir to combine. Pour in the egg mixture and cook, stirring constantly for 1-3 minutes or until the eggs are set but still creamy. Serve immediately.

Egg And Bacon Naan Pizzas

Preparation time: 20 minutes
Cooking time: 21 minutes
Nutrition facts (per serving): Calories 170 (4% fiber, 13% sodium, 17% fat)

Ingredients (16 servings)
4 pieces of naan bread (pizza style)
1 1/2 cups shredded mozzarella cheese
1/2 cup of grated cheddar cheese
1 tablespoon of unsalted butter
4 strips of bacon
1 small tomato
4 chives
1 avocado (large)
4 eggs
Salt
Black pepper

Preparation
Preheat the oven to 400 F. Line 2 large baking trays with parchment paper. Put aside. Line a large plate with paper towels. Put aside. Place the butter in a microwave-safe bowl. Microwave over 600W (350 F) for 20-30 seconds, or until melted. Place the naan pizza bread on one of the baking trays. Using a small pastry brush, brush the surface of each naan pizza bread with melted butter. Place the bacon strips on the other baking tray. Cut the tomato into cubes. Remove and discard the seeds. Put aside. Finely chop the chives and put aside. Cut the avocado in half. Remove and discard the pit.

Use a spoon to gently peel the avocado pulp from the skin and lay it flat on the cutting board. Discard the peels. Cut the avocado crosswise into small ¼ slices.

Sprinkle an equal amount of the mozzarella and cheddar cheese over each naan bread. Gently break an egg in the center of each naan pizza bread. Place both baking trays on the center rack of the oven. Bake for 15-17 minutes, until the cheese is golden, the egg white is cooked, and the bacon is brown and crisp. If the bacon is not fully cooked, remove the naan pizza bread and cook the bacon for 3-4 minutes more.

Remove the baking trays from the oven. Place the bacon on the paper towel-lined dinner plate to drain. Spread an equal amount of avocado slices and diced tomatoes on each pizza. Crumble the bacon with clean hands and sprinkle it evenly over the pizzas. Sprinkle the chopped chives over the pizzas. Season the top of the pizzas with salt and pepper. Cut into slices and serve.

Egg And Cheese Casserole

Preparation time: 35 minutes
Cooking time: 48 minutes
Nutrition facts (per serving): 170 Calories (24% protein, fat 18%, fat 18%)

Ingredients (11 servings)
8 ounces of grated cheddar cheese
12 eggs
1/3 cup of whole milk
1 teaspoon of salt
1/4 teaspoon black pepper

Preparation
Preheat the oven to 350 F. Spray a 9x13" baking dish with nonstick cooking spray. Beat the milk, eggs, salt, and black pepper in a large mixing bowl. Add grated cheese. Fold with a rubber spatula until the cheese is evenly distributed.

Pour the mixture into the prepared baking dish. Place the dish on the center rack of the preheated oven. Bake the casserole for 40-45 minutes, until golden brown on top and a toothpick in the center comes out clean. Remove the pan from the oven. Let the casserole cool for at least 12 minutes before serving. Cut the casserole into squares and place it on a plate with a large spoon.

Polish Fluffy Waffle

Preparation time: 5 minutes
Cooking time: 10 minutes
Nutrition Facts (per serving): 417 Calories (Protein 9g, Fat 18g, Fiber 1g)

Ingredients

1 1/2 cups of milk

6 tablespoons unsalted butter, melted

2 cups all-purpose flour

4 tablespoons granulated sugar

4 teaspoons baking powder

1/2 teaspoon of salt

2 eggs

1 teaspoon vanilla extract

Preparation

Preheat the waffle iron. Coat gently with non-stick cooking spray. In a large bowl combine the flour, sugar, baking powder, and salt. Use the back of a spoon to make a well in the center. Beat the two eggs in the milk until well combined. Pour the milk/egg mixture, butter and vanilla into the well of the dry ingredients and beat until blended. The batter will be a bit lumpy, so don't over-mix. Spoon the batter into the preheated waffle iron and cook 3 minutes or until the waffles are golden brown and crispy. Serve immediately or place on a wire rack to cool. Store leftovers in an airtight bag in the freezer.

Polish American Gingerbread Pan

Preparation time: 15 minutes
Cooking time: 15 minutes
Nutrition Facts (per serving): 326 Calories (21 g fat, 16 g carbohydrates, 18 g protein)

Ingredients (6 servings)
1 bell pepper, red, chopped
1 bell pepper, green, chopped
1 large onion, finely chopped
1 pound fresh Polish white sausage
2 cups of leftover *kluski* (or 2 large boiled potatoes, sliced)
6 large eggs
1/2 cup cheese, grated
Salt and pepper to taste

Preparation
Heat the oven to 350 F. Remove the meat from the Polish sausage casings and place it in a large cast-iron skillet. Add the bell pepper and onion and cook until the sausage is cooked through and the vegetables are tender. Add 2 tablespoons of butter.

Add *kluski* or potatoes and heat through. Add the eggs and stir over medium-high heat, stirring constantly until the eggs are cooked to your taste. Adjust herbs and sprinkle with cheese, cover the surface completely and place the skillet in the oven until the cheese has melted.

Polish Babka Bread

Preparation time: 3 hours
Cooking time: 25 minutes
Nutrition Facts (per serving): 328 Calories (Protein 7g, Fat 10g, Cholesterol 10g)

Ingredients (1 serving)
1/2 cup unsalted butter, softened
1 cup of milk, scalded
4 cups of all-purpose flour
1/2 cup of sugar
4 egg yolks
1 teaspoon of salt
1 cup of raisins, optional
1 packet of yeast
1/4 cup of lukewarm water
1 egg lightly beaten
2 tablespoons of water

Preparation
Sprinkle the yeast over your lukewarm water, stir a little and then let it sit. To scald milk, pour the milk into a small saucepan and heat over high heat until the milk is almost boiling. Remove from heat and let cool. Meanwhile, in a mixing bowl with the paddle attachment, combine butter and sugar. Add salt to the egg yolks and mix well, add to the butter and sugar mixture. Scrape the sides and blend to incorporate.

Add your activated yeast mixture and mix well. Alternately add flour and roasted milk in batches until incorporated. Mix for about 7-8 minutes until the dough is smooth. If you're using raisins, mix them in at this point.

Remove the dough from the paddle and into the bowl of the mixer. Cover the bowl with a towel and place in a warm, dark place for 1 1/2 hours to rise. Another option is to turn on the oven for a moment until it reached 100 F and then turned it off again. Then place a covered bowl inside with the door closed to let it rise.

Generously butter two large loaf pans. Remove the risen dough and knock it down. Cut the dough into two equal pieces. Place the dough in the two prepared loaf pans. Spread the dough with your fingers so that it evenly covers the bottom of your pan. Brush the top of each dough with egg wash.

Cover each loaf pan with a towel and place it in a dark, warm place to rise a second time. Let rise for about 52-57 minutes. Remove towel. Place the loaves in the preheated oven to 355 F. Bake for 26-32 minutes. Remove from the oven and let cool in the pan for 7 minutes. Then remove the loaves from the pan onto a cooling rack. Otherwise, condensation will build upon the bottom of the loaves. Once the loaves have cooled enough, slice them and serve.

Homemade Kolache

Preparation time: 4 hours
Cooking time: 15 minutes
Nutrition Facts (per serving): 263 Calories (total fat 102 g, cholesterol 249 mg)

Ingredients (6 servings)
2 eggs
1/2 cup plus 1/4 cup melted butter
1 packet of yeast
1 cup of warm milk
1/4 cup sugar
3 cups of flour
1 teaspoon of salt
Fillings of your choice

Preparation
In a large bowl, combine yeast, warm milk, sugar, and 1 cup of flour. Mix well, cover, and let it rise until doubled in size for at least 35 minutes. In a separate bowl mix eggs, 1/2 cup of melted butter, and salt. Add to yeast mixture. Mix in 2 ½ cups of flour or a little more. The dough should be soft and moist. Knead for 11 minutes. Place in a greased bowl and let rise for at least 70 minutes or until doubled.

Knock down the dough and pull out pieces, about 3-inch in size. Place them on a greased baking sheet and flatten them to about 5 inches wide. Smaller for the jam-covered, larger for the ones that will be filled). Brush with melted butter and place the filling in the center.

Pull up the sides to cover the filling and squeeze together to seal. Turn over, so the sealed side is at the bottom. Let rise for 30 minutes. For jam, let Kolaches rise for 30 minutes, then make holes in the top and fill with spoons of jam. Bake for 13 to 15 minutes in the preheated oven at 375 F. Brush them with more melted butter when they come out of the oven.

Polish Apple Pancakes

Preparation time: 75 minutes
Cooking time: 30 minutes
Nutrition facts: 171 Calories (Fat 1.71g, Carbs 12.6g, Protein 1.97g)

Ingredients (6 servings)

2 eggs, beaten
1 tablespoon of salted butter, melted and cooled slightly
2½ cups unbleached all-purpose flour
1 tablespoon of sugar
2 teaspoons active dry yeast
1/4 teaspoon of salt
1½ cup lukewarm milk
2 large apples
½ cup rapeseed oil (for frying)
Icing sugar

Preparation

In a bowl, combine the sugar, flour, yeast, and salt. Add the melted butter, milk and eggs. Mix until the mixture is moist and thick. Cover the batter and place in a warm, draft-free place to rise for 85 minutes. Peel, core, and dice the apples towards the end of the rising time. Once the dough has risen, stir in the diced apples.

Add 2 tablespoons of oil to cover the bottom of a 12-inch sauté pan. Heat the oil over medium heat. Spoon the batter into the hot pan and spread it as thinly as possible with the thick pieces of apple in between. Bake the pancakes for 3 minutes until the bottom is golden brown. Turn the pancakes over and cook on the other side for 2-3 minutes, until golden brown; then remove the pancakes from the pan and place on a paper-lined plate.

Repeat the process with the remaining dough, adding more oil as necessary. Keep the finished pancakes warm while you cook the rest. In general, pancakes are best crispy and fresh from the pan, so try to serve them straight from the pan. Sprinkle with icing sugar before serving.

Baked Polish Paczki

Preparation time: 4 hours
Cooking time: 10 minutes
Nutrition Facts (per serving): 329 Calories (Carbs 49g, Fat 12g, Protein 6g)

Ingredients (24 servings)

2 eggs
4 egg yolks
2 tablespoons of brandy
1½ cup lukewarm milk
1 ½ tablespoon of active dry yeast
1/3 cup unsalted butter, softened
¼ cup of sugar
1 teaspoon of salt
6 cups unbleached all-purpose flour
1 cup smooth jam, pastry cream or lemon curd
1 cup icing sugar or granulated sugar

Preparation

Add the warm milk in a small bowl. Sprinkle the yeast over the milk and let it rest for 5 minutes so that the yeast becomes soft and foamy. Beat the butter and sugar in an electric mixer with a paddle attachment until pale and fluffy. Add the brandy, eggs, yolks and salt. Beat until combined and fluffy. With the mixer on low speed, add one-third of the milk mixture, alternating with flour, until you have added 5 cups flour. Switch from the paddle attachment to dough hooks when the dough starts to come together. Mix on medium speed until the dough comes together, adding more flour if necessary. The dough should be soft and sticky, but not runny.

Increase the speed of the mixer to medium and knead the dough for 6-7 minutes until smooth and shiny. Remove the dough from the dough hooks and cover the dough in the bowl with a damp tea towel. Let the dough rise in a warm, draft-free place for 90 minutes or until doubled in size.

When the dough has risen, place it on a well-floured work surface and knock it down. Roll out the dough to ½ inch thickness. Use 3-inch circular cookie cutter to cut circles from the dough. Roll again and cut if necessary, until all dough is cut. Place the rounds on a baking tray lined with parchment paper. Cover the circles lightly with your damp kitchen towel and let them rise for about 45 minutes or until puffy and nearly doubled.

By the end of the rising time, heat your oven to 375 F and bake the donuts for 7-10 minutes in the preheated oven, until a toothpick in the center of one of the donuts comes out clean. Let the donuts cool on the baking tray for 2-3 minutes before placing them on a wire rack. If you are filling your paczki, do this after 10 minutes or once they are cool enough to handle. Fill it with the desired jam or custard filling. Insert the tip of the pastry bag into the center of the paczki as far as possible. Gently squeeze the pastry bag while slowly pulling the tip out of the donut. You will feel the paczki gain weight as you fill them with about 2 tablespoons of the filling.

If you are using granulated sugar to sugar your donuts, roll them in the sugar while they are still warm so that the sugar sticks. If you're using powdered sugar to sugar your donuts, wait for them to cool completely before rolling them in powdered sugar.

Sausage With Vegetables

Preparation time: 12 minutes
Cooking time: 30 minutes
Nutrition Facts (per serving): 346 Calories (Fat 24g, Protein 18g)

Ingredients: (4 servings)
1/2 medium onion, chopped
1/2 medium green pepper, seeded, chopped
1 1/2 cups sliced mushrooms
2 medium Yukon Gold potatoes, peeled, cut into 1/2-inch cubes
2 tablespoons of unsalted butter
6 ounces smoked sausage, sliced 1/4-inch thick
1/4 cup of whole milk
6 eggs
Salt and pepper

Preparation
Place the potatoes and 2 teaspoons salt in a large, deep saucepan and add enough water to cover the potatoes 1-inch above them. Bring to a boil over high heat and simmer for 7-10 minutes or until potatoes are just tender. Drain and wipe the skillet away.

Melt butter in the same skillet over 325 F. Add sausage pieces. Cook, stirring occasionally until browned on both sides, about 4 minutes. Transfer to a bowl with a slotted spoon. Add vegetables to the pan and season with salt and pepper. Cook over medium to high heat, stirring occasionally for 8-9 minutes or until mushrooms are browned and vegetables are tender.

Beat the eggs with milk in a medium bowl. Season with salt and pepper. Add sausage and potatoes to vegetables in a skillet and stir to combine. Pour in the egg mixture and cook, stirring constantly for 1-2 minutes or until the eggs are set but still creamy. Serve immediately.

SOUPS

Polish Beet Soup
(Barszcz Czysty Czerwony)

Preparation time: 15 minutes
Cooking time: 45 minutes
Nutrition facts (per serving): 117 Calories (1 g fat, 22 g carbohydrates, 8 g protein)

Ingredients (4 servings)
4 whole beets
4 cups of beef or vegetable stock
1 clove of garlic, finely chopped
1 teaspoon of sugar
2 tablespoons fresh lemon juice or 1 tablespoon red wine vinegar
Salt and black pepper
Boiled potatoes to serve

Preparation
Heat the oven to 400 F. Wrap the beets in aluminum foil and roast until tender, about 35 to 45 minutes. When cool enough to handle, peel and cut into strips or julienne. In a saucepan, bring meat or vegetable stock to a boil. Add chopped beets, sugar, salt, garlic, lemon juice and pepper to taste. Simmer for 12 minutes. Serve hot with boiled potatoes.

Polish Ryemeal Soup with Sausage (Żurek)

Preparation time: 30 minutes
Cooking time: 45 minutes
Nutrition Facts (per serving): 463 Calories (13 g fat, 75 g carbs, 15 g protein)

Ingredients (6 servings)
3/4 cup rye flour
2 cups of water, boiled
1/2 pound peeled and chopped soup vegetables (celeriac, leeks, carrots, parsnips,)
6 cups of water
1/2 pound of fresh (white) Polish sausage (*biały kiełbasa*)
1 pound potatoes, peeled and cut into 1-inch pieces
2 cups of rye meal sour
1 heaped tablespoon of all-purpose flour mixed with 4 tablespoons of water
1 clove of garlic crushed with 1/2 teaspoon of salt
3 hard-boiled eggs

Preparation
To make the ryemeal sour, bring 2 cups water to a boil and then let it cool down to lukewarm. In a bowl, mix ¾ cup rye flour with lukewarm water. Pour into a glass jar or ceramic bowl large enough for the mixture to expand. Cover with cheesecloth and leave in a warm place for 5 days. This should make 2 cups or enough for the soup. If not used immediately, the sour can be kept covered in the refrigerator for up to 6 days.

In a stockpot, bring soup vegetables and 6 cups of water to a boil. Reduce heat and simmer for 35 minutes. Add sausage, return to a boil, reduce heat and cook for another 30 minutes. Remove sausage from soup, slice when cool enough to handle, and set aside. Pour the stock through a sieve and press the vegetables to get as much flavor as possible. Discard the vegetables, scoop the fat from the stock and return the stock to a clean stockpot.

Add the potatoes and ryemeal sour to the stock; add salt if necessary. Bring to a boil, reduce heat and cook until potatoes are al dente.

Add the garlic-salt paste, flour-water mixture and reserved sliced cooked sausage. Wisk to incorporate well and make sure there are no lumps. Bring the soup to a boil. Simmer and cook until the potatoes are tender. Serve in heated bowls with half a hard-boiled egg.

Polish White Borscht Soup (Biały Barszcz)

Preparation time: 10 minutes
Cooking time: 30 minutes
Nutrition facts (per serving): 623 Calories (37 g fat, 37 g carbs, 35 g protein)

Ingredients (7 servings)
6 cups sausage cooking water (fat removed)
1 garlic clove, finely chopped
2 cups of sour cream
1/4 cup all-purpose flour
1 link white Polish *kiełbasa* sausage, casing removed, sliced 1/4-inch thick
7 potatoes, peeled, chopped, and boiled
7 hard-boiled sliced eggs
Salt and ground black pepper to taste
7 slices of light or dark rye bread

Preparation
In a saucepan, add the garlic, sausage and water. Bring to a boil, reduce heat and simmer, partially covered, for 6 minutes. In a small bowl, mix the sour cream and flour. Temper the sour cream with a little hot sausage water; then add the sour cream mixture to the pan, stirring until thick. Add a tablespoon of vinegar or sugar if desired. The soup should have a nice sour taste. Add eggs, sausages and potatoes to the pan and heat well. Season with salt and pepper. In 7 heated bowls, tear the rye bread into bite-sized pieces and add it to the bowls. Spoon the hot soup over the bread.

Polish Borscht (Barszcz)

Preparation time: 10 minutes
Cooking time: 20 minutes
Nutrition Facts: 147 Calories (Protein 6.5g, Fat 4.9g, Fiber 4.1g)

Ingredients (3 servings)
4 beets, peeled and cut into 1-inch pieces
1 bay leaf
1 tablespoon of salted butter
4 cloves of garlic, chopped
2 whole allspice berries
1 onion, diced
2 carrots cut into rounds
1 celery stalk, cut into cubes
4 cups of beef stock
2 tablespoons of apple cider vinegar
1 teaspoon sugar
1/4 teaspoons ground black pepper
Pinch of salt

Preparation
Melt butter in a large stockpot. Add garlic and onion. Cook over medium to high heat for 6 minutes or until onion is soft. Add carrots, allspice, beets, celery and bay leaf. Stir with butter. Add stock and bring to a boil. Cook 15 minutes or until vegetables are tender and then remove the pan from the heat. Stir the pepper, sugar, vinegar and salt into the soup. Taste and add more salt and pepper if needed.

Chilled Beet Soup (Chlodnik)

Preparation time: 35 minutes
Cooking time: 45 minutes
Nutrition facts (per serving): 194 Calories (Protein 12.7g, Fat 5.7 g, Fiber 1.8 g)

Ingredients (5 servings)

½ pound beets, peeled and grated
1 small cucumber cut into cubes
1 cup vegetable stock, low in sodium
1 cup buttermilk
¾ cup plain low-fat yogurt or low-fat sour cream
4 hard-boiled eggs, peeled and quartered
¼ cup lemon juice
2 tablespoons of fresh dill
1 tablespoon fresh chives
1 teaspoon of salt
3 tablespoons of sugar (optional)

Preparation

Place the grated beets in a 2-quart saucepan. Fill the pan with water until the beets are about 1 inch covered and heat, uncovered, over medium heat for 37-45 minutes. Steam, but do not boil. When finished, remove the pan from the heat and refrigerate until cool. This can be done a day or two in advance. When ready to make the soup, add yogurt, vegetable stock, lemon juice, buttermilk, diced cucumbers, dill, chives and salt to the chilled beet and water mixture. Add sugar if necessary. Serve cold, garnished with hard-boiled eggs.

Polish Chicken Soup (Rasol)

Preparation time: 10 minutes
Cooking time: 2 hours
Nutrition facts (per serving): 230 Calories (Protein 13g, Fat 5g, Carbs 31g)

Ingredients (8 servings)
5 chicken parts with bones
1 small piece of beef bone
2 yellow onions
1/4 cup cabbage
5 carrots
1 parsnip
6 feather parsley and more for serving
1 tablespoon of apple cider vinegar
3 bay leaves
9 cups of water
Celeriac
Leeks
5 allspice berries
1/2 pounds thin noodles cooked according to instructions
Salt and pepper to taste

Preparation
Wash, peel and chop all the vegetables. Heat a frying pan and add the unpeeled onions to get some burn marks. Add beef bone, chicken pieces, allspice, and bay leaves in a large saucepan. Add vegetables and fill the pan with water. Add vinegar and about 1 tablespoon of salt.

Simmer for 2 hours on 210 F, but don't boil it. While cooking, scoop off anything that has accumulated on the surface a few times. Check for seasoning, add salt and pepper as desired or chicken cubes. Cook the noodles separately according to the instructions. Once cooked, rinse with cold water to remove starch. Add noodles to the bowls. Remove the pieces of chicken from the stock, remove the meat from the bones, cut it into pieces, and put it into the bowls. Spoon the soup into bowls. Add chopped parsley and serve.

SALADS

Polish Potato Salad
With Eggs And Pickles

Preparation time: 15 minutes
Cooking time: 30 minutes
Nutrition Facts (per serving): 244 Calories (Protein 8g, Fat 13g, Fiber 4g)

Ingredients (8 servings)
4 eggs
3 medium pickles in brine
8 small/medium gold potatoes
1/2 small red onion, chopped
3 green onions chopped
2 tablespoons of dill, chives, parsley
1/2 cup mayonnaise
1/2 cup plain Greek yogurt
2 tablespoons sour cream
1 tablespoon Dijon Mustard
Salt and pepper to taste

Preparation
Clean the potatoes and put them in a pan of water. Cook until tender when pierced with a fork; about 20-30 minutes.

Boil the water for the eggs in a saucepan. Once the water is boiling, add a pinch of salt and put the eggs in the boiling water. Cook for 9-11 minutes. Once cooked, set the potatoes and eggs aside and let them cool. Meanwhile, add onions, finely chopped gherkins and herbs in a bowl. In a separate bowl, combine sour cream, mayo, yogurt, mustard, salt, and pepper. When the potatoes and eggs have cooled, peel and chop them and put them in the bowl with the pickles, onions, and herbs. Add sauce and mix.

Traditional Polish Salad
(Salatka Jarzynowa)

Preparation time: 20 minutes
Cooking time: 30 minutes
Nutrition Facts (per serving): 359 Calories (Protein 12 g, Fat 54 g, Fiber 18 g)

Ingredients (8 servings)
1 celeriac
1 onion or the white part of the leek
3 potatoes
2 parsley roots
4 carrots
4 large fermented cucumbers
1 can of sweet peas
1 apple (optional)
6 boiled eggs
10 tablespoons of mayonnaise
Salt and pepper

Preparation
Peel carrot, celeriac, potatoes, and parsley roots. Cook them until soft. Boil the eggs. Chop all the vegetables except the peas. Mix all the ingredients and add mayonnaise. Mix the Polish salad well and add salt and pepper as needed. Put in the fridge and serve cold.

Polish Cucumber Salad (Mizeria)

Preparation time: 3 minutes
Cooking time: 10 minutes
Nutrition facts (per serving): 89 Calories (Protein 2 g, Fat 7 g, Fiber 6 g)

Ingredients (4 Servings)
11 ounces cucumber, rinsed, peeled or unpeeled

Creamy dressing
1/2 cup sour cream
1 tablespoon lemon juice
1.2 tablespoons dill and chives, finely chopped
Sea salt and pepper to taste

Oil dressing
2 tablespoons of good quality vegetable or mild-tasting olive oil
1 1/2 tablespoons lemon juice
1 tablespoon dill and chives (optional) finely chopped
Sea salt and pepper to taste

Preparation
Make the creamy dressing by combining lemon juice, sour cream, dill, salt and paper and stirring well. If you choose to make the oil dressing, simply combine the oil and lemon juice and set aside (add the herbs to the salad just before serving).

Cut the cucumber into 2-3mm thick slices. Combine with your chosen dressing and enjoy it.

Another method of preparing the cucumber is to slice it very thinly with a vegetable cutter. Season with salt and stir well, then place in a colander for 11-13 minutes to lightly brine and allow the cucumber to release liquid. After 10 minutes, squeeze out the remaining moisture and combine the cucumber with your favorite dressing. Serve.

Creamy Cucumber Salad

Preparation time: 15 minutes
Nutrition Facts (per serving): 34 Calories (Fat 1g, Protein 6g, Fiber 4g)

Ingredients (6 servings)
3 cups thinly sliced cucumbers
1/2 cup thinly sliced onions
1/2 cup of plain Greek yogurt
1 tablespoon chopped fresh dill
1 tablespoon of fresh lemon juice
1 teaspoon of sweetener
1/2 teaspoon of garlic powder
Salt and pepper to taste

Preparation
Cut the cucumber and onion into thin slices. If possible, use a mandolin because it is quick and easy. Add the cucumber and onions to a bowl with the remaining ingredients. Stir until well blended. Serve chilled or at room temperature.

Mother's Potato Salad

Preparation time: 20 minutes
Cooking time: 20 minutes
Nutrition Facts (per serving): 256 Calories (Protein 9g, Fat 12g, Fiber 3g)

Ingredients (8 servings)
4 medium salad potatoes unpeeled
5 tablespoon thick yogurt
5 tablespoon mayonnaise
2 medium carrots unpeeled
6 small pickles, finely chopped
4 eggs hard-boiled
2 apples
1 tablespoon mustard
Fine sea salt and pepper to taste

Preparation
Put the potatoes and carrots in a saucepan, add water and bring to a boil. Simmer until cooked, but don't overcook. You can cook the eggs in the same pan and take them out after 7-9 minutes. Drain and set aside to cool, peel and chop ingredients into small cubes and place in a large bowl. Chop the pickles and add them in the bowl. Peel and core the apples, quarter and finely chop. Combine with the salad. Add the mustard, yogurt, mayonnaise and herbs to the mixture and stir gently but thoroughly. Refrigerate 1 hour before serving.

Traditional Krakow Salad

Preparation time: 15 minutes
Cooking time: 10 minutes
Nutrition Fact (per servings): 547 Calories (Protein 18 g, Fiber 14 g, Fat 1g)

Ingredients (6 servings)
1 cup sour cream
2 tablespoons mayonnaise
5 cucumbers, thinly sliced
4 radishes, thinly sliced
3 tablespoons green onions, finely chopped
2 tablespoons fresh dill, chopped
2 tablespoons freshly squeezed lemon juice
2 tablespoons salt
1/2 tablespoon sugar, optional

Preparation
Place the cucumber slices in a large colander that rests on a bowl or in the sink. Sprinkle with salt and set aside, let the juices drain from the cucumber for 16-20 minutes. In a large bowl, beat sour cream, sugar, mayonnaise and lemon juice. Add cucumbers, radishes, green onions, and dill and mix everything well.

Warsaw Cucumber Salad

Preparation time: 15 minutes
Nutrition Facts (per serving): 52 Calories (Protein 1.5 g, Carbohydrates 6.3 g, Cholesterol 7.9 mg)

Ingredients (6 servings)
½ cup low-fat sour cream
2 tablespoons fresh lemon juice
2 tablespoons chopped fresh dill
3 medium seedless cucumbers, halved lengthwise and thinly sliced crosswise
½ cup thinly sliced red onion
1 pinch of coarse salt and ground black pepper to taste

Preparation
Mix sour cream, lemon juice, and dill in a bowl. Add cucumbers and onion; stir to combine. Season with salt and black pepper.

Beet Salad

Preparation time: 90 minutes
Cooking time: 15 minutes
Nutrition Facts (per serving): 33 Calories (Protein 8g, Fiber 5g, Fat 0g)

Ingredients (4 servings)
3 medium beets
1/2 teaspoon of sugar
1/2 teaspoon of white vinegar
1/4 of an onion
1 teaspoon of oil
Juice from 1/2 large lemon
Pinch of salt

Preparation
Preheat oven to 350 F. Cut beet stems and scrub to clean. Bake covered for about 1 hour. Take it out and set it aside to cool. Once cooled, peel and grate on the largest size of a box grater. Add oil, lemon juice, chopped onion, salt, and sugar. Mix and put in the fridge to cool before serving.

Polish Vegetable Salad

Preparation time: 20 minutes
Cooking time: 20 minutes
Nutrition facts (per serving): 158 Calories (Protein 90g, Fat 4g, Fiber 12g)

Ingredients (8 servings)

8 small potatoes, boiled and cut into small pieces
1/2 cup mayonnaise
2 teaspoons lemon juice
1 can peas, drained
1 can of carrots, drained and cut into small pieces
1 teaspoon salt
1/2 teaspoons pepper
1/4 teaspoons paprika
1 stalk celery, cut into very small pieces
1 apple, peeled and cored, chopped into small pieces
3 pickles, chopped into very small pieces
3 tablespoons sour cream
1 teaspoons mustard
3 tablespoons fresh dill

Preparation

Peel and cook potatoes. Place very small pieces of potato in a mixing bowl. Add carrots, peas, mayonnaise, lemon juice, salt, pepper, celery, apple, pickles, sour cream, dill, and mustard. You may want to add some ingredients according to your taste, before serving.

Beetroot With Horseradish

Preparation time: 30 minutes
Cooking time: 45 minutes
Nutrition facts (per serving): 26 Calories, (Fat 0 g, Fiber 1 g)

Ingredients (9 servings)
1 pound beets
1 horseradish root, finely grated
1 teaspoons salt, to taste
1 lemon, squeezed, to taste
1 teaspoons vinegar, to taste
2 teaspoons of sugar, to taste

Preparation
Prepare the beets by boiling them gently with their skin on for about an hour or until tender. Do not overcook. While the beets are cooling, peel the horseradish and finely grate them in a bowl. Once cooled, peel and grate the beets in a medium bowl. Combine beets and horseradish. Add the remaining ingredients to taste. Mix well and refrigerate overnight for the best flavor.

MAIN DISHES

Horseradish With Beets
(Polish Ćwikła)

Preparation time: 30 minutes
Nutrition Facts (per serving): 45 Calories (Fiber 2.8g, Protein 1.61g, Fat 0.17g)

Ingredients (3 servings)
1 teaspoon white vinegar
1 teaspoon brown sugar
2 cups grated fresh horseradish root or purchased horseradish
1/4 teaspoon salt
1 pound beets (cooked, peeled, cooled, and grated)

Preparation
In a bowl, combine vinegar, brown sugar, horseradish, and salt until well blended. Add grated beets and mix well. Pack in clean sterilized jars and store in the refrigerator for up to 2 weeks.

Polish Jellied Pigs' Feet (Zimne Nogi)

Preparation time: 30 minutes
Cooking time: 2 hours
Nutrition facts (per serving): 335 Calories (Fat 12g, Carbs 41g, Protein 15g)

Ingredients (6 servings)
1 1/2 pounds pork feet, split, trimmed and cleaned
3 allspice berries to taste
2 finely chopped garlic cloves
1 tablespoon salt
1 cup soup vegetables (peeled onion, celery, etc.)
1 bay leaf
6 black peppercorns
1 pound lean pork (such as loin)
1 tablespoon gelatin (dissolved in 1/2 cup of cold water)
1/2 teaspoon marjoram
Salt and black pepper to taste

Preparation
Rinse the pork feet and pat them dry with kitchen paper. Place pork feet and just enough water in a large pot to barely cover them. Add bay leaf, peppercorns, allspice, garlic, peeled soup vegetables and salt. Bring to a boil and remove any foam. Add the pork loin, return to a boil, reduce heat, cover and simmer for 1 1/2 to 2 hours or until foot flesh falls off the bones.

Remove the meat from the water and deboned it. Pour the stock through gauze and put it in a clean pan. Remove the cooked carrots from the soup vegetables and chop the meat and carrots into small pieces. Return diced meat and carrots to the broth, along with marjoram and more crushed garlic, and salt and pepper, if desired. Bring to a boil and add the dissolved gelatin, stirring until well incorporated.

Let cool slightly and pour into molds or bowls. Put in the fridge overnight. When ready to serve, unmold it on a serving platter or individual plates. Garnish with leafy greens or parsley, serve with vinegar, horseradish, lemon, and marinated mushrooms.

Polish Pork Ribs (Żeberka Wieprzowe)

Preparation time: 20 minutes
Cooking time: 2 hours
Nutrition Facts (per serving): 814 calories (Fat 41 g, Carbohydrates 25 g, Protein 84 g)

Ingredients (6 servings)
2 cups unsweetened applesauce
2 tablespoons brown sugar
4 pounds country-style pork ribs (1 1/2 inches thick cut)
2 cloves garlic, finely chopped
1 pound sauerkraut, drained and rinsed if necessary
1 tablespoon caraway seeds
A few pinches of salt and black pepper

Preparation
Heat the oven to 450 F. Rinse the pork ribs and pat them dry with kitchen paper. Rub the ribs all over with garlic, salt, and pepper. Place ribs meat-side down in a shallow roasting pan and roast without a lid for 20 minutes. Reduce oven temperature to 250 F. Turn ribs over so that they are now meat-side up.

In a large bowl, combine sauerkraut, applesauce, brown sugar, and caraway seeds and mix well. Pour over the pork ribs. Cover the casserole and cook for 2 hours or until the meat is tender. Serve with green vegetables and dill sauce.

Potato Drop Dumplings (Kartoflane Kluski)

Preparation time: 10 minutes
Cooking time: 20 minutes
Nutrition Facts (per serving): 103 calories (Fat 3 g fat, Carbohydrates 17 g, Protein 3 g)

Ingredients (8 servings)
1 cup of flour
1 cup of milk
1 large potato, peeled and finely grated
1/2 teaspoon salt
1/8 teaspoon pepper

Preparation
Bring a pot of salted water to a boil. Meanwhile, in a medium bowl, combine flour, milk, grated potato, salt, and pepper into a thick paste. Dip a teaspoon in the boiling water, then dip it in the dough mixture; scoop half a teaspoon and slide it into the gently boiling water. Continue until all the dumpling dough is used. Simmer for about 18-20 minutes. Dumplings should taste tender. Drain in a colander and serve as a side dish.

Chef's Pierogi Lasagna

Preparation time: 60 minutes
Cooking time: 70 minutes
Nutrition facts (per serving): 688 calories (Fat 55g fat, Carbohydrates 22g, Protein 29g)

Ingredients (12 servings)
Dough
1 egg
3/4 cup sour cream (and more for garnish)
8 tablespoons softened unsalted butter
1 tablespoon chopped chives (and more for garnish)
1 teaspoon salt
2 cups all-purpose flour (and more for rolling dough)

Filling
2 pounds russet potatoes, peeled and cut into large pieces
1 cup whipped cream, warmed
1 1/2 cups Gruyere or similar cheese, shredded
1 1/2 cups farmer's cheese, shredded
8 tablespoons cold butter, cubed
2 large yellow onions, thinly sliced
1 tablespoon of olive oil
1 pound bacon, chopped
Salt and black pepper to taste

Preparation
Combine egg, butter, sour cream, chives, and salt with hands in a bowl. Don't overwork it, even if the mixture is not purely uniform. Add flour

and mix with your hands until a dough form. Wrap it in plastic and put the dough in the refrigerator for at least three hours.

Place the potatoes in a large saucepan. Cover with two inches of cold water and bring to a boil. Season the water generously with salt. Reduce heat to simmer and cook until a knife pierces the potatoes easily. Drain the potatoes and return them to the same pan. Puree and slowly mix in the warm cream and cold butter. Season with salt and pepper and set aside.

Heat olive oil in a skillet over 325 F. Cook bacon until crispy, about 10 minutes. Transfer to a plate with a slotted spoon.

Reduce heat to medium, put the onions in the pan, and cover with bacon fat. Season with salt and pepper. Cook, stirring frequently until the onions are caramelized and sweet. Let cool.

Butter a 13 x 9-inch baking dish or metal pan. Heat oven to 350 F. Roll out pierogi dough with a rolling pin to a 1/8 inch thick rectangle. Cut into 4x13-inch strips and re-roll the leftovers as needed. About 16 strips will be made.

Place crispy bacon, mashed potatoes, cheeses, caramelized onions and pasta strips on a work surface. Place a layer of dough strips on the bottom of the buttered baking dish, slightly overlapping the edges. Spread a 1/2-inch layer of potatoes over the dough. Top with some caramelized onions, bacon, and a pinch of *Gruyère* and farmer's cheese. Repeat layers to use the remaining ingredients. Finish with a dough layer, followed by *Gruyère* and farmer's cheese. Season with pepper.

Cook 45 minutes or until the lasagna is bubbly and the cheese on top is golden brown. Let rest for 16 to 20 minutes and then serve with a dollop of sour cream and a pinch of chives.

Polish Cabbage And Noodles

Preparation time: 5 minutes
Cooking time: 65 minutes
Nutrition Facts (per serving): 437 Calories (Carbohydrates 73.7 g, Protein 15.2g, Fat 10.3 g, Fiber 8.3 g)

Ingredients (2 servings)
2 cups of cabbage, cut into 1-inch strips
1 cup sauerkraut drained
1 (4 ounces) can mushroom, drained
1 teaspoon caraway seeds
1 small onion, chopped
¼ cup of water
1 bay leaf
½ teaspoons thyme
¼ teaspoon oregano
½ teaspoons paprika powder
6 ounces small noodles, dry (egg noodles are the closest to traditional Polish noodles)
1/8 teaspoons ground black pepper
¾ teaspoon salt
¼ cup sour cream

Preparation
Heat the onions with 2 tablespoons of water over medium heat in a large skillet. Cover and cook for 33-37 minutes or until dark brown and caramelized, checking regularly and add water if necessary, to avoid scalding. Add the remaining ingredients except for noodles and sour cream. Simmer for 24-26 minutes on low heat or until the cabbage is cooked. Bring

some water to boil in a medium saucepan. Add the noodles and cook 8-10 minutes, until al dente. Drain and set aside. Remove the cabbage mixture from the heat. Add sour cream and mix well. Add drained noodles and mix until well blended. Top with parsley before serving.

Polish Sausage And Sauerkraut

Preparation time: 15 minutes
Cooking time: 20 minutes
Nutrition Facts (per serving): 353 Calories (Fat 4.5 g, Protein 9.8 g, Fiber 7.8 g)

Ingredients (2 servings)

1 1/2 pounds (about 2 large) russet potatoes cut into ½ inch cubes
1 pound Polish sausage cut into 1/2 inch slices
1 onion, sliced and cut into 1-inch pieces
1 cup sauerkraut
1 tablespoon unsalted butter
½ teaspoons ground black pepper
¼ teaspoon salt

Preparation

In a large saucepan, cover the potato cubes with water and cook until just tender, 6-8 minutes. Drain the potatoes and set them aside. In a non-stick frying pan, add the sausages and half a cup of water. Cook over medium heat until the water evaporates. Then fry the sausage for 7-9 minutes or until golden brown. Remove from the pan.

Heat 1 teaspoon of butter in the pan, if needed. Add the onions and sauerkraut and cook until dry and golden brown, 4-6 minutes. Shift the onion mixture to one side of the pan. Add the remaining 2 teaspoons of butter to the empty side of the pan and add the boiled potatoes. Gently scoop the potatoes into the hot butter before mixing all the ingredients in the pan. Fry the mixture, stirring every minute or two until the potatoes are golden brown. After 5-6 minutes, when potatoes are starting to turn crispy, taste the hash and season with salt and pepper to taste. Return the sausage to the pan and heat for 2-3 minutes. Serve.

Polish Style Stuffed Zucchini

Preparation time: 15 minutes
Cooking time: 45 minutes
Nutrition facts (per serving): 296 Calories (Protein 21.6g, Fat 9.9g, Cholesterol 91mg)

Ingredients (4 servings)

½ c white rice, dry
1 teaspoon of oil
1 onion, diced
2 large zucchinis
½ pounds ground beef (90% lean)
1 egg
1 teaspoon paprika powder
1 teaspoon garlic powder
1 teaspoon thyme
1 teaspoon marjoram
¾ teaspoon salt
¾ teaspoons ground white pepper
¼ cup breadcrumbs

Preparation

Preheat your oven to 350 F. Bring 1 cup water to a boil and add rice. Cook for 8-11 minutes, until rice just starts to soften. Drain the rice and set aside. In the meantime, heat oil in a skillet and sauté the onions over medium-high heat for 2-4 minutes or until golden brown. Remove from heat and set aside. Slice the zucchini lengthways and scrape out the core, creating a boat with about ½ inch of flesh on all sides.

In a large bowl, combine egg, ground beef, sautéed onions, pre-cooked rice and spices. Fill the zucchini boats with the filling and top with breadcrumbs. Place the zucchini boats on an aluminum foil-lined baking pan and bake on 165 F, uncovered for 40-50 minutes or until the top is golden brown. Serve.

Pork Balls With Creamy Dill Sauce (Pulpety)

Preparation time: 10 minutes
Cooking time: 20 minutes
Nutrition facts (per serving): 678 Calories (Fat 42g, Protein 51g, Fiber 1g)

Ingredients (3 servings)
1 stale bread bun
1/2 cup milk,
1 pound ground pork
1 onion
1 egg
1/2 bunch fresh dill
1 teaspoon salt, to taste
2 pints vegetable stock, can be replaced with chicken stock
2 teaspoons butter
2 teaspoons flour
1/2 bunch fresh dill
Pepper, to taste

Preparation
Pour milk over the bun or brioche and let it rest for 15 minutes. Mix the ground beef with an egg in a large bowl. Squeeze out the milk from the bun and crumble. Add the bread to the meat mixture. Season with salt and pepper. Add finely grated onion and half a bunch of chopped dill to the mix. Mix everything with hands. Shape walnut-sized meatballs. Heat the vegetable stock. Bring the stock to a boil and drop the meatballs one by one into the liquid. Reduce heat to low and cook for 22-25 minutes.

Mix flour with butter, add a few spoons of stock from the stove. Slowly add this mixture back to the pan and mix gently with a spoon until the sauce thickens. Add the chopped dill and turn off the heat. Serve with side dishes of your choice.

Bigos Stew

Preparation time: 25 minutes
Cooking time: 2,5 hours
Nutrition Facts (per serving): 385 Calories (Protein 14.7 g, Carbohydrates 7.8 g, Cholesterol 74.9 mg)

Ingredients (6 serving)

2 ounces butter
½ teaspoon caraway seeds
11 ounces lean pork belly, diced
1 onion, sliced
1 teaspoon juniper berries, crushed
1 tablespoon brown sugar
1 pound sauerkraut
Half a white cabbage, shredded
7 ounces freshly cut tomatoes
1 ½ cup chicken or beef stock
1 ounces dried mushrooms
11 ounces smoked Polish sausage removed from the casing
1 apple, grated
Pinch sea salt
Freshly ground black pepper

Preparation

Melt the butter in a frying pan. Add the onion and cook over 250 F until the onion is soft and translucent. Sprinkle with the juniper berries and caraway seeds and then add the pork. Sprinkle with the brown sugar.

Turn the heat on high for 5 minutes and turn the meat so that it browns well. Drain the sauerkraut well and rinse if you want to reduce the vinegar flavor.

Add to the frying pan with the white cabbage and chopped tomatoes and pour over the stock. Simmer for 28-35 minutes. Soak the dried mushrooms in warm water, enough to cover them. When they have softened, drain them and add their soaking liquid to the frying pan. Chop the mushrooms and add them to the pan along with the sausage and apple. Simmer for another 1 ½ hours and serve.

Kielbasa With Beer

Preparation time: 10 minutes
Cooking time: 6 hours
Nutrition Facts (per serving): 387 Calories (Protein 14.7 g, Carbohydrates 7.8 g, Cholesterol 74.9 mg, Sodium 1490.5 mg)

Ingredients (8 servings)

2 pounds of kielbasa sausage, cut into 1-inch pieces
1 (12 fluid ounce) can or bottle of beer
1 (20 ounces) can of sauerkraut, drained

Preparation

Combine sausage, beer, and sauerkraut in a slow cooker. Cook over low heat for 6 hours until the meat is tender and plump. Serve.

Polish Bean And Sausage Stew

Preparation time: 20 minutes
Cooking time: 1 hour 5 minutes

Nutrition Facts (per serving): 817 Calories (Protein 47g, Carbohydrates 89.4g, Cholesterol 73.5mg)

Ingredients (4 servings)
2 ½ cups dry cannellini beans
1 tablespoon vegetable oil
10 slices bacon, cubed
½ pound ring kielbasa sausage, diced
2 medium onions, chopped
2 bay leaves
1 tablespoon butter
1 tablespoon all-purpose flour
1 teaspoon paprika
4 whole allspice berries
1 can diced tomatoes
1 tablespoon dried marjoram, to taste
1 clove garlic, chopped
1 pinch of salt and ground black pepper, to taste

Preparation
Place the cannellini beans in a large bowl and cover with a few inches of cold water; soak for at least 8 hours. Drain and add to a large saucepan. Cover with fresh water and cook over medium heat for 55-60 minutes or until beans are tender.

Heat oil in a skillet over medium-high heat while the beans are cooking. Add bacon and sausage and cook for 6-9 minutes or until brown. Put the meat in a bowl and keep some of the fat in the pan. Cook onions in the reserved fat for 6-9 minutes or until brown. Add to the bowl with the meat.

Stir the meat mixture, bay leaves, and allspice into the cooked beans and bring to the boil. Add tomatoes, marjoram, garlic, salt, and pepper and simmer for 10 to 15 minutes. Add water if there is not enough liquid in the skillet.

Melt butter in a small saucepan over 150 F, add flour and stir into a paste. Remove from heat and add to the stew; stir in the paprika. Simmer for 13-16 minutes or until the stew has thickened. Serve.

Kielbasa And Cabbage

Preparation time: 10 minutes
Cooking time: 30 minutes

Nutrition facts (per serving): 373 Calories (Protein 17.2g,
Carbohydrates 20.2g, Cholesterol 63.1mg)

Ingredients (per serving)
6 slices of bacon
2 teaspoons of chopped garlic
¼ teaspoon ground red pepper flakes
3 teaspoons of caraway seeds
¼ cup of water
2 tablespoons of white sugar
1 onion, chopped
1 large head cabbage, cut into small wedges
1 pound of Polish kielbasa

Preparation
In a large skillet, fry bacon over medium-high heat until browned, turning
once. Remove the bacon from the pan and put it on kitchen paper to drain.
In the same pan, stir in onions, sugar, water, garlic, red pepper flakes,
seasoned salt, and caraway seeds. Add cabbage and stir gently. Cover and
cook over medium heat for 11 to 14 minutes. Add kielbasa to the pan and
cook covered for an additional 14-16 minutes. Crumble the bacon on top
and serve warm.

Kielbasa And Vegetables

Preparation time: 15 minutes
Cooking time: 1 hour
Nutrition Facts: (per serving): 643 Calories (Protein 22.2 g, Carbohydrates 35.6 g, Cholesterol 116.3 mg)

Ingredients (4 servings)

1 package frozen mixed vegetables, thawed
¼ cup butter, cut into pieces
1 tablespoon lemon pepper
¼ cup grated Cheddar cheese
4 small potatoes, peeled and cut into pieces
1 package Polish beef sausage, cut into 1/4 inch slices

Preparation

Preheat the oven to 380 F. Spread the mixed frozen vegetables over the bottom of a lightly greased 9 x 12-inch baking dish. Mix in potatoes and sausage, and slice butter cubes evenly over the mixture. Sprinkle with lemon pepper and cover with aluminum foil. Bake in a preheated oven for 50 minutes. Open the foil carefully, spread the cheese on top and let it melt.

Polish Chop Suey

Preparation time: 10 minutes
Cooking time: 1 hour 10 minutes
Nutrition Facts (per serving): 618 Calories (Protein 23.1g, Carbs 50 g, Cholesterol 121.9 mg)

Ingredients (6 servings)
1 (16 ounces) package of *kluski* noodles
2 (16 ounces) packages of kielbasa sausage
1 can (10.75 ounces) condensed cream of mushroom soup
1 (1 ounce) package of dry onion soup mix
3 (10.75 ounces) cans of water
1 can (14.5 ounces) sauerkraut, drained

Preparation
Preheat the oven to 350 F. Bring a large pot of lightly salted water to a boil. Cook kluski noodles in the boiling water. Stir occasionally for 4-6 minutes or until tender but firm. Drain. Heat a skillet over medium heat. Cook sausages in the pan for 4-6 minutes or until brown. Cut into bite-sized pieces.

Stir the mushroom soup, onion soup mix, and water together in a large baking dish; add *kluski* noodles, sausage, and sauerkraut. Cover the dish with aluminum foil. Bake in the preheated oven for 70 to 90 minutes. Serve.

Halushki

Preparation time: 10 minutes
Cooking time: 20 minutes
Nutrition Facts (per serving): 698 Calories (Protein 22.3 g protein, 68.7 g carbohydrates, 114.2 mg cholesterol)

Ingredients (6 servings)

1 (16 ounces) package of egg noodles
1 head cabbage, sliced
1 pound of bacon
1 onion, diced
1 pinch of salt and ground black pepper to taste

Preparation

Cut the bacon into small pieces with scissors and cook in a large skillet over medium-high heat for 9-10 minutes or until crispy. Stir often. Cook and stir onion with bacon for 4-7 minutes or until translucent. Set bacon and onion aside and leave the drippings in the pan.

Bring a large pot of lightly salted water to a boil. Cook egg noodles in the boiling water, stirring occasionally, for 4-6 minutes or until tender but firm. Drain.

Return the bacon and onion mixture to the large skillet, add the cabbage and stir the cabbage until covered in bacon drippings. Cover the skillet and cook for 11-13 minutes or until the cabbage is tender. Stir in the noodles carefully and season with salt and black pepper.

Polish Meatballs

Preparation time: 30 minutes
Cooking time: 15 minutes
Nutrition Facts (per serving): 342 Calories (Protein 28.6 g, Carbohydrates 14.7 g, Cholesterol 134.7 mg)

Ingredients (4 servings)

2 onions, roughly chopped
40 crackers saltine crackers, crushed
¾ cup of dry breadcrumbs
½ can evaporate milk
6 celery stalks, roughly chopped
2 ½ pounds ground veal
2 ½ pounds ground pork
1 can (10.75 ounces) condensed cream of mushroom soup
3 eggs
4 teaspoons salt, or to taste
1 teaspoon dried marjoram
1 teaspoon dried onion flakes
¾ teaspoon ground black pepper

Preparation

Preheat the oven to 380 F. Mix the celery and onions in a large frying pan. In a large bowl, mix the veal and pork thoroughly with your hands. Lightly stir in the evaporated milk, breadcrumbs, mushroom soup, cracker crumbs, eggs, pepper, salt, marjoram and onion flakes. From the mixture into medium-sized meatballs, dip your hands in water between making the balls. Carefully place the meatballs in the frying pan, top it with the onions and celery, and cover the pan with foil.

Bake for 1 hour in the preheated oven and remove foil. Carefully separate the meatballs where they are stuck together and return the pan to the oven until the meatballs are brown, turning every 15 minutes until they are done. Serve.

Polish Breaded Pork Chops
(Kotlety Schabowy)

Preparation time: 15 minutes
Cooking time: 15 minutes
Nutrition facts (per serving): 865 Calories (Fat 76g fat, Carbs 55g, Protein 40g)

Ingredients (4 servings)
1 egg, beaten with 1 teaspoon of water
2 cups breadcrumbs
1 cup shortening or vegetable oil
4 boneless pork chops (or 1-pound pork tenderloin)
Salt and black pepper to taste
2 cups flour

Preparation
Cut off fat and gristle when using pork chops. If using pork tenderloin, cut off the fat and cut into 4 equal pieces. Pound pork between two pieces of plastic wrap to 1/4-inch thickness. Season both sides with salt and pepper.

Dredge cutlets in flour, then the egg-water mixture, then breadcrumbs or panko crumbs. Let the cutlets dry for 15 minutes before frying them. Heat shortening or oil to a depth of 1/2 inch in a skillet.

Fry the cutlets 6 to 8 minutes per side or until golden brown. Serve hot with applesauce, boiled potatoes and a green vegetable.

Stuffed Cabbage Rolls (Golabki)

Preparation time: 30 minutes
Cooking time: 70 minutes
Nutrition Facts (per serving): 395 Calories (Protein 20.1 g, Carbohydrates 41.5 g, Cholesterol 60.8 mg)

Ingredients (8 servings)
1 pound ground beef
1/2 pound ground pork
1 1/2 cups cooked rice
1 whole head cabbage, about 4 pounds
1 large onion, chopped
2 tablespoons butter
1 teaspoon finely chopped garlic
1 teaspoon salt
1/4 teaspoon black pepper
1 cup beef stock
Sour cream for garnish

Preparation
Remove the core from the head of cabbage and put it in a saucepan of boiling, salted water. Cover and cook for 3 minutes or until soft enough to pull off individual leaves. Meanwhile, fry the chopped onion in butter until translucent. Let cool.

Drain the cabbage. Pull individual cabbage leaves off and drain in a colander. Keep 18 leaves for this recipe and coarsely chop the remaining leaves and place them on the bottom of an ovenproof dish with a lid or a Dutch oven. When the leaves in the colander have cooled enough to handle, use a paring knife to trim the tough stalk from each without cutting the leaves all the way through.

Mix cooled onions with rice, beef, pork, garlic, salt, and black pepper until well blended. Do not mix too long or the meat will become tough. Place a 1/2 cup meat mixture at the bottom of each cabbage leaf.

Flip the bottom of the cabbage leaf up and over the meat to cover it completely. Make a nice package and roll. First, turn the right edge of the cabbage leaf to the center and then to the left until you have a package that looks like an envelope. Then roll the cabbage package away from you until you have a tube shape, such as an eggroll or burrito.

Place the cabbage rolls in an ovenproof dish or Dutch oven on top of the chopped cabbage and season each layer with salt and pepper.

Drizzle the beef stock over the cabbage rolls, cover with the lid and bake in a pre-heated oven at 350 F for one hour or until the cabbage is tender and the meat cooked through. Serve with sour cream.

Stuffed Cabbage Rolls
With Tomato Sauce

Preparation time: 35 minutes
Cooking time: 50 minutes
Nutrition Facts (per serving): 349 Calories (Fat 10 g fat, Carbs 48 g, Protein 19 g)

Ingredients (6 servings)
Stuffed cabbage rolls
1/2 pound ground pork
3/4 teaspoon salt
1 cup buckwheat groats
2 cups of water3 pound cabbage, cored
1 large onion, finely chopped
3 tablespoons oil
1/4 teaspoon pepper

Sauce
1 small onion, finely chopped
2 tablespoons tomato paste
1/2 teaspoon salt
1/8 teaspoon pepper
1/4 teaspoon sugar
1 tablespoon butter
2 tablespoons flour
1 cup chicken stock

Preparation

In a large saucepan, bring buckwheat groats and 2 cups of water to a boil. Reduce heat, cover, and simmer for 11-13 minutes until groats are al dente. Drain. Place the entire head of cabbage in a saucepan filled with boiling salted water. Cover and cook for 4-5 minutes or until soft enough to peel individual leaves. Drain in a colander and let cool.

Keep 18 leaves and trim the thick part of the midrib from all of them. Coarsely chop the remaining cabbage.

In a frying pan, fry the chopped onion in oil until golden brown. Transfer to a bowl and add pork, cooked and cooled buckwheat groats, salt, and pepper. Place ½ cup of meat mixture in the center on each cabbage leaf. Fold the bottom of the cabbage up and away from you. Fold in the sides and roll like an eggroll. Place some of the coarsely chopped cabbage in the bottom of a large roasting pan with a lid or Dutch oven and add the rolls in layers if necessary. Top with the remaining coarsely chopped cabbage. Add 1 cup of boiling salted water and cook on low to medium heat for 43-47 minutes on the stovetop. Alternatively, cook for 50 minutes in a 355 F preheated oven.

To make the tomato sauce, fry the chopped onion in butter until translucent. Stir in the flour and whisk in the cold stock. Add tomato paste and cook over low heat until thick. Season with pepper, salt and sugar. Serve over cabbage rolls.

Breaded Pork Tenderloin

Preparation time: 30 minutes
Cooking time: 30 minutes
Nutrition Facts: 339 Calories (Fat 20 g, Cholesterol 110 mg, Sodium 327 mg)

Ingredients

1 pound pork tenderloin
1/3 cup all-purpose flour
1 egg, beaten
4 tablespoons canola oil
1/3 cup corn flour
1/2 teaspoon salt
1/4 teaspoon pepper
Ranch or barbecue sauce, optional

Preparation

Cut pork crosswise into 1/2-inch slices. In a bowl, combine flour, corn flour, salt, and pepper. Place the egg in a separate bowl. Dip the pork in the egg and then in the flour mixture and press to help the coating adhere. In a large skillet, heat 2 tablespoons of oil over medium-high heat. Add half of the pork; cook 3-4 minutes each side or until a thermometer reads 145 F. Drain on paper towels. Wipe the skillet clean and repeat with remaining oil and pork. Serve with sauce if desired.

Polish Pizza

Preparation time: 15 minutes
Cooking time: 40 minutes
Nutrition Facts (per serving): 453 Calories (Fats 25g, Carbs 35g)

Ingredients (4 servings)

2½ tablespoons olive oil
5 ounces ripe cheddar cheese, coarsely grated
2 ounces salami slices
3 spring onions, trimmed and cut at an angle
5 ounces pickled cucumbers in a jar, sliced
Coarse ground Black pepper

Dough

13 ounces white bread flour
1½ teaspoons dried quick yeast
2 tablespoon olive oil, plus a little extra for greasing
1 cup lukewarm water
¾ teaspoons salt

Preparation

For the dough, put everything in the bowl of a kitchen mixer with the dough hook attached and knead on medium speed for 8 minutes or until soft and elastic. Place the dough in a well-oiled bowl, cover, and let rise in a warm place for 45-55 minutes or until almost double in size.

Heat oven to 430 F. Generously grease an 8" x 12" baking pan with olive oil, add the dough and use your fingers to spread it evenly to fill the pan. Brush the dough with two tablespoons of oil, bake for 11-13 minutes, then remove from the oven and spread the cheese evenly over the top, pushing it slightly into the dough with your fingers.

Return to the oven for 4-6 minutes, then remove and spread evenly with the salami, spring onions, and pickled cucumbers. Return to the oven for a final five minutes; remove from the oven, place on a wooden cutting board, and drizzle with the remaining half a tablespoon of oil. Finish with a generous sprinkle of black pepper, slice, and serve.

Potato Pancakes

Preparation time: 10 minutes
Cooking time: 15 minutes
Nutrition facts (per serving): 258 calories (Sodium 168 mg, Fat 3.25 g)

Ingredients

1 (20-ounce) package of refrigerated hash brown potatoes, crumbled
1/4 cup freshly grated Parmesan cheese
2 tablespoons all-purpose flour
2 garlic cloves, chopped
2 eggs, beaten
2 tablespoons olive oil
3 green onions, thinly sliced
1/4 teaspoon cayenne pepper
Salt and freshly ground black pepper, to taste

Preparation

In a large bowl, mix flour, potatoes, Parmesan, garlic, eggs, green onions, and cayenne pepper. Season with salt and pepper. Heat olive oil in a skillet over low to medium heat. For each pancake, scoop tablespoons of the batter into the pan, flatten with a spatula and cook 3 minutes or until the bottom is a nice golden brown. Flip and cook on the other side, about 2 minutes longer. Serve.

Polish Street Food (Zapiekanka)

Preparation time: 10 minutes
Cooking time: 5 minutes
Nutrition facts (per serving): 462 calories (Fat 36 g, Saturated fat 19 g, Cholesterol 92 g)

Ingredients (6 servings)
Baguette Bread cut in half and cut lengthwise
1-2 tablespoons butter
2 cups white mushrooms, sliced
1/2 small white onion sliced
3 cups freshly grated cheddar cheese
Ketchup for garnish

Preparation
Preheat to 300F. Melt the butter in a skillet over 200 F and sauté the mushrooms and onions until soft and cooked through. Season with salt and pepper.

Spread the cooked mushrooms and onion evenly over each half of the baguette to cover the cut side of the bread. Sprinkle with freshly grated cheddar cheese. Roast 6 minutes or until the cheese is completely melted. Drizzle with ketchup before serving.

Poznan Cabbage Rolls

Preparation time: 1 hour
Cooking time: 90 minutes
Nutrition facts (per serving): 311 Calories (Fat 12 g, Cholesterol 45g, Saturated fat 5g)

Ingredients (22 servings)
1 large or 2 small heads of cabbage
1 tablespoon olive oil
1 cup diced onion
2 cloves garlic, chopped
2 large mushrooms, chopped
1 pound ground sirloin steak
3/4 cup uncooked long-grain rice
1/4 cup chopped parsley
1 cup Pomi-strained tomatoes (or canned tomato paste)
1 1/2 teaspoons salt
Pepper to taste
3/4 cup liquid (beef stock or water)

Preparation
Bring a pot of water to the boil. Cut the center core out of the cabbage and place it core down in boiling water. Cover and simmer for 11-13 minutes. While the cabbage is simmering, heat the oil in the pan over medium-high heat and fry onion and garlic for 4-6 minutes or until brown. Add mushrooms and cook for 2-3 more minutes. Transfer the mixture to a large bowl to cool. Place the cabbage on a rimmed baking sheet and leave the water in the pan. Slowly remove the leaves from the cabbage. Set aside the best 16 unbroken leaves and trim the thick stalk in the center to make rolling easier. Set aside any leftover broken or small cabbage leaves.

Preheat the oven to 350 F. Add rice, meat, parsley, tomato, salt, and pepper to the cooled onion mixture. Combine well. Place about 1/2 cup of filling on each cabbage leave, roll, and place seam side down in a 13 x 9-inch pan. Pour liquid used to boil the cabbage over the rolls and put some leftover cabbage leaves on top. Cover the pan tightly with foil and bake for at least 90 minutes. Remove from oven and rest for 30 minutes or more.

Poznan Cabbage And Noodles

Preparation time: 10 minutes
Cooking time: 10 minutes
Nutrition Facts (per serving): 1,420 calories (Carbs 153 g, Fat 79 g, Protein 37 g)

Ingredients (3 servings)
1 tablespoon butter and 1 tablespoon of olive oil
1 1/2 cups chopped onion
3/4 teaspoon salt and pepper to taste
3 ounces egg noodles (about 1 1/2 cups uncooked)
4 cups chopped cabbage
1/2 teaspoon caraway seeds
1 tablespoon butter

Preparation
Boil the water for the noodles. In a large saucepan, melt butter and oil over medium-high heat and fry the onion for 4-5 minutes or until golden brown. When onions are cooked, start cooking the noodles. Add cabbage, caraway seeds, salt, and pepper to the onions. Boil and stir for 7-8 minutes. Remove from heat and stir in the drained noodles and 1 tablespoon of butter.

Lublin Pierogi

Preparation time: 90 minutes
Cooking time: 30 minutes
Nutrition Facts (per serving): 210 Calories (Fat 2 g, Protein 0 g)

Ingredients
Filling
1 garlic clove, crushed
3 ounces low-fat cream cheese (1/3 cup)
1 1/2 pounds potatoes (2 large russet)
2 teaspoons olive oil
1/2 cup finely chopped onion
1/2 teaspoon salt
Pepper to taste

Dough
1 egg
2 1/2 cups all-purpose flour
1/2 teaspoon salt
1/4 cup reduced-fat sour cream
2/3 cup of water

Preparation
Filling
Place the peeled, quartered potatoes in a saucepan of cold salted water. Bring to the boil and cook until tender. Meanwhile, brown onions and garlic in oil on medium-low for 10 min. Drain and mash the potatoes, add garlic and onion, cream cheese, salt and pepper. Set aside to cool. If desired, shape into 1 tablespoon mounds.

Dough

Combine flour and salt in a bowl. Make a well and add egg, sour cream and water. Combine with a spoon. Place on a well-floured plate and knead 50 turns (if necessary with a scraper) until smooth. Cover with a towel or inverted bowl and let rest for at least 15 minutes.

Divide the dough into three. Keeping extra dough covered, roll out each section 1/8 inch thick and add flour as needed. Cut 3-inch circles and save leftover dough. Fill each circle with about a tablespoon of potato mixture, fold them into a half-circle, and squeeze the edges tightly. Set them aside on a towel dusted with flour. Place pierogis in boiling salted water, stirring to keep them separate, and cook for about 4 minutes or until they come up to the surface, then another 45 seconds to a minute. Remove with a slotted spoon and place on an oiled baking tray. Serve.

Custard Filled Pączki

Preparation time: 30 minutes
Cooking time: 10 minutes
Nutrition Facts (per serving): 170 Calories (Total fat 29%, Saturated fat 50%, Trans fat 0%)

Ingredients (12 servings)
1 1/2 cups all-purpose flour
1/4 cup sugar
1/4 teaspoon salt
2 teaspoons yeast (instant or regular)
1/4 cup extra flour
1 tablespoon melted butter
1/3 cup sugar for coating
1 cup homemade custard
2/3 cup milk, heated to 120° F
3 tablespoons vegetable oil
2 egg yolks
1/2 teaspoon vanilla

Custard Filling
1/4 cup sugar
1 egg yolk
4 teaspoons cornstarch
1 cup of milk

Preparation
Place flour, salt, yeast, and sugar in a large bowl. Stir in the warm milk, followed by oil, egg yolks, and vanilla. Beat for 3 minutes with an electric

mixer. Stir in enough flour until the dough holds together. Knead on a floured surface 5 to 7 minutes, cover with plastic sheeting and let rest for 12 minutes.

Custard Filling

Combine sugar and cornstarch in a small saucepan. Slowly stir in the milk and egg yolks. Bring to a boil. Cook and stir for about 1-2 minutes. Spread on a plate and let stand, undisturbed, to cool thoroughly before use - refrigerate if necessary.

Line a large baking tray with parchment paper. Roll the dough on a floured surface 1/2-inch thick. Cut circles with a 2 1/2 inch round cutter dipped in flour. Roll up the leftovers and use them again. Place the circles on a baking tray, cover with a towel and let rise in a warm place for about 45 minutes. During this time, preheat the oven to 375 F. If the circles are puffy, almost doubled in size, bake for 10 minutes. Melt butter and put 1/3 cup of sugar in a plastic bag.

Remove from the oven and brush all of them while warm (top and sides) with melted butter. Immediately place them in the bag with sugar and cover them completely with the sugar. Let them cool before filling them.

Scoop the custard filling into a piping bag with a long tip; press it into the side of the bun and push the custard in the bun while slowly pulling the tip of the piping bag from the bun. Or cut a slit in the side of the bun and add the custard with a spoon. Serve.

Polish Potato Gnocchi (Kluski)

Preparation time: 45 minutes
Cooking time: 25 minutes
Nutrition facts (per serving): 236 Calories (Fat 1g, Cholesterol 40g, Sodium 47mg)

Ingredients (6 servings)
1 1/2 pounds russet potatoes
2 cups all-purpose flour
1 egg
1/2 teaspoon salt

Preparation
Cut peeled potatoes into 2-inch pieces and put them in a saucepan of cold salted water. Bring to boil, cover and simmer for 13-16 minutes or until tender. Drain and then mash the potatoes while still hot in a large bowl.

Stir flour into hot potatoes, followed by egg and salt. Place them on a floured work surface and knead for about a minute to obtain a smooth dough. If necessary, lift with a scraper. Don't overwork the dough. Cut the dough into 8 parts. Roll each section into a rope about 18 inches long. With a scraper or knife, cut each rope into 1-inch pieces (about 20 pieces per rope). Drop in boiling salted water, stirring so they don't stick. Cook for about 2-3 minutes (no more). When they rise to the top, wait for 16-20 seconds before removing with a slotted spoon. Serve.

Cottage Cheese With Noodles

Preparation time: 10 minutes
Cooking time: 20 minutes
Nutrition facts (per serving): 543 Calories (Protein 20.8g, Carbs 57.2g, Cholesterol 123mg)

Ingredients (6 servings)

½ cup butter
½ cup sour cream
1 cup cottage cheese
1 onion, diced
1 (16 ounces) package of egg noodles
¼ teaspoon of sea salt
¼ teaspoon ground black pepper

Preparation

Melt butter in a saucepan over medium to high heat. Cook and stir onion in melted butter for 5-8 minutes or until soft. Bring a large pot of lightly salted water to a boil. Cook egg noodles in the boiling water, stirring occasionally, for 6 minutes or until tender but firm. Drain and return to the pot. Stir butter and onion mixture, cottage cheese, sour cream, sea salt, and black pepper into the noodles. Put the pan on low heat, cook and stir for about 5 minutes or until heated through and warm. Serve.

Fish With Root Vegetables

Preparation time: 30 minutes
Cooking time: 60 minutes
Nutrition facts (per serving): 362.4 Calories (Protein 26.5g,
Carbohydrates 25.6 g, Cholesterol 114.7 mg)

Ingredients (4 servings)

2 large eggs, beaten
¾ cup all-purpose flour
1 pinch of salt and black pepper to taste
2 pounds firm white fish fillets (cod, haddock, or halibut), cut to 1-inch slices
¾ cup vegetable oil, divided
¼ cup of vegetable oil
2 onions, halved and thinly sliced
2 carrots, peeled and coarsely grated
½ celeriac, peeled and coarsely grated
4 tablespoons tomato paste
1 large parsnip, peeled and coarsely grated

Preparation

Place the eggs and flour in 2 bowls. Season the eggs with salt and pepper. Dip the pieces of fish in the beaten eggs and then dredge them in the flour. Heat 3/4 cup of vegetable oil in a deep skillet over medium-high heat until hot. Add the fish in batches and cook 5-8 minutes per batch or until golden brown on both sides. Remove the fish from the pan and set aside.

Heat the remaining 1/4 cup of oil in a separate skillet and sauté the onions for 6 minutes or until soft and translucent. Add celeriac, carrots, parsnips and mix well. Add water and season with salt and pepper. Cover and simmer for 32-35 minutes over low heat until vegetables are tender. Check and add more water if the mixture becomes too dry. Stir in the tomato paste and simmer for an additional 6 minutes. Layer vegetables and baked fish in a round serving dish, starting and ending with vegetables.

Grandma's Polish Perogies

Preparation time: 1 hour
Cooking time: 1 hour
Nutrition facts (per serving): 281.3 Calories (Protein 8 g, Carbohydrates 37.6 g)

Ingredients (20 servings)

4 ½ cups all-purpose flour

2 eggs

1 egg yolk

8 potatoes, peeled and diced

1 cup grated Cheddar cheese

2 tablespoons processed cheese sauce

2 tablespoons vegetable oil

2 teaspoons salt

2 tablespoons butter, melted

2 cups sour cream

1 dash onion salt to taste

1 pinch of salt and pepper to taste

Preparation

In a bowl, stir together the flour and salt. Beat the butter, sour cream, eggs, egg yolk, and oil in a separate bowl. Stir the wet ingredients into the flour until well blended. Cover the bowl with a towel and let stand for 16 to 22 minutes.

Place the potatoes in a saucepan and cover them with enough water to submerge. Bring to the boil and cook for 16 minutes or until tender. Drain and mash with grated cheese and cheese sauce while still hot. Season with onion salt, salt, and pepper. Set aside to cool.

Divide the dough into two balls. Roll out piece by piece on a lightly floured work surface until thin enough to work with, but not too thin to tear. Cut into circles with a cookie cutter or a glass. Brush a little water around the edges of the circles and put some filling in the center. Fold the circles into semicircles and press to seal the edges. Place perogies on a baking tray and freeze. Once frozen, transfer to freezer bags or containers.

Bring a large pot of lightly salted water to a boil. Drop perogies one by one into the boiling water. They are done when they float to the top. Do not overcook.

Polish Kiełbasa Sausage
(Biała Kielbasa)

Preparation time: 30 minutes
Cooking time: 40 minutes
Nutrition facts (per serving): 274 Calories (Carbohydrates 0%, Fat 23 g, Protein 14 g)

Ingredients (16 servings)

4 pounds boneless, well-marbled pork shoulder (cut into 1-inch wide strips)
1/2 cup of cold water
2 garlic cloves, pressed
4 teaspoons of salt
1 teaspoon of black pepper
1 teaspoon of marjoram leaf
14-foot pork intestines for casing (rinsed three times and chilled)

Preparation

Keep the meat chilled until ready to grind. Grind the strips of meat in a manual or electric grinder using the medium plate. Place the meat in a large bowl.

Combine ground meat with garlic, water, salt, pepper, and marjoram. To make sure the spices are good, fry a small burger and taste. Keep the ground beef mixture in the refrigerator for at least two hours before filling.

Remove the casings from the refrigerator and tie one end. Lightly coat the hopper with cooking spray. Slide the other end of the casing over the opening of the funnel. Make sure that it is not twisted and that the opening is centered on the funnel. Keep pushing the rest of the casing onto the funnel until you reach the knot.

Start pushing the meat into the casing with one hand and use the other hand to control the thickness of the sausage while it is being extruded. Sausage will shrink when it cooks, so it is important to make a thick sausage.

Continue to extrude until the casing is finished. Tie a knot at that end. You can leave the sausage in a large spiral or twist it at 5- to 6-inch intervals to make links. Keep refrigerated and covered for up to 2 days until ready to cook.

Pierce sausage along the length of the link to release air bubbles, or it will explode in the cooking water. Place sausage in a large saucepan and cover with water. Bring to a boil over medium heat. Reduce heat to low and simmer uncovered for 32 minutes, or until internal temperature reaches 160 F. You can then brown it in a 350 F oven or a pan for 16 to 22 minutes. Remove to a serving platter and enjoy with homemade horseradish.

Beef And Cabbage (Lazy Golumpki)

Preparation time: 15 minutes

Cooking time: 1 hour 20 minutes

Nutrition fact (per serving): 287 Calories (Protein 14.4 g, Carbohydrates 36.7 g, Cholesterol 34.8 mg)

Ingredients (8 servings)

1 cup green cabbage, cut into bite-sized pieces

2 cups of water

1 cup white rice

1 pound ground beef

1 teaspoon salt

1 teaspoon dried parsley

1 teaspoon dried parsley

¼ teaspoon onion powder

1/8 teaspoon ground black pepper

1 can (10.75 ounces) condensed tomato soup

1 (32 ounces) container of crushed tomatoes

Preparation

Cook cabbage in a stockpot, 11 to 16 minutes. Drain well. Heat a large skillet over high heat. Cook and stir beef in the hot skillet for 6 to 8 minutes or until brown and crumbly. Drain the fat and throw it away. Mix salt, parsley, onion powder, and black pepper with minced meat. In a saucepan, bring water and rice to a boil. Reduce heat to low, cover, and simmer until rice is tender and liquid is absorbed 22 to 25 minutes. Stir the tomato soup and the crushed tomatoes together in a bowl.

Preheat the oven to 355 F. Combine beef, cabbage, rice, and tomato mixture in a bowl; transfer to a 9 x13 inch baking dish. Bake in the preheated oven for 43-45 minutes or until bubbly. Serve.

Wedding Hen
(Ślub z Kurczaka)

Preparation time: 95 minutes
Cooking time: 15 minutes
Nutrition fact (per serving): 567 Calories (Fat 17g, Protein 360g, Fiber 90g)

Ingredients (3 servings)
1 chicken cut into pieces, washed and pat dry
1 tablespoon paprika
Salt and pepper
Vegetable oil
1 large onion per 4 servings, thinly sliced

Preparation
Heat the oven to 450 F. Season the chicken with salt, pepper, and paprika. Rub everything with oil. Place in an uncovered roasting pan and bake for 16 minutes, turning over. Reduce heat to 350 F. Spread the sliced onions over the chicken. Cover and cook for 65 to 70 minutes, basting regularly with stock and/or pan dripping until golden brown, and an instant-read thermometer in the thickest part of the dark meat registers are cut 165 F.

The chicken fillets cook faster than the legs and thighs. When the breasts reach 165 F, remove them to a platter and cover loosely with aluminum foil while the other meat is done cooking.

Polish Beef Roulade (Zrazy)

Preparation time: 30 minutes
Cooking time: 60 minutes
Nutrition facts (per serving): 640 Calories (Fat 9g, Carbs 106g, Protein 34g)

Ingredients (4 servings)
8 sandwich steaks, trimmed
1 tablespoon granular mustard
2 dill pickles cut into thin strips
4 ounces ham, cut into thin strips
1 cup beef stock
4 tablespoons white wine
1 tablespoon tomato paste
2 green onions cut into thin strips
4 tablespoons canola oil
2 tablespoons all-purpose flour
1 teaspoon salt (or to taste)
1/2 teaspoon pepper (or to taste)

Preparation
Pound the sandwich steaks to 1/8th inch thick. Spread a thin layer of mustard over each steak and divide the pickles, ham, and onion over the steaks. Fold the sides in half and roll like stuffed cabbage. Secure with a toothpick if necessary.

Heat oil in a large frying pan and brown beef rolls on all sides. Remove and store meat. Add flour to the pan and cook until lightly browned to a roux.

Stir in the stock, wine, tomato paste, salt, and pepper. Bring to a boil and simmer for 1-2 minutes. Return the beef rolls to the pan and top with some sauce. Cover and simmer over low heat for 45-50 minutes. Add more liquid if necessary while cooking.

When the rolls are cooked, place them on a serving platter and remove the toothpicks, if used, and spoon over the sauce. Decorate with a dollop sour cream and chopped parsley.

Polish Meatloaf Stuffed With Mushrooms

Preparation time: 20 minutes
Cooking time: 60 minutes
Nutrition Facts (per serving): 344 Calories (Fat 18 g, Carbohydrates 12 g, Protein 31 g)

Ingredients (6 servings)
Mushroom filling
1/2 ounces dried mushrooms
1 1/2 cups of water
4 ounces fresh mushrooms, chopped
1 onion, finely chopped
2 tablespoons butter
2 tablespoons breadcrumbs
Salt and black pepper to taste

Meatloaf
1 slice white bread (stale)
1/2 cup milk
3/4 pound ground beef
1/2 pound lean ground pork
1 onion, finely chopped
1 egg, lightly beaten
A few pinches salt and black pepper

Preparation
Place the mushrooms in a heatproof bowl and pour boiling water over it. Let it steep for 2-3 hours. Transfer mushrooms and liquid (taking care not

to disturb the sediment in the bottom of the soaking bowl) to a saucepan and cook until tender and most of the liquid has evaporated. Chop and reserve.

In a skillet, cook fresh mushrooms and medium onion in butter, covered, about 16-18 minutes. Add the dried mushrooms, leave the lid off, and continue cooking until the liquid evaporates. Remove from heat and add breadcrumbs, salt, and pepper to taste. Reserve.

In a large bowl, soak the bread in milk until soft. Add beef, pork, onion, egg, salt, and pepper and mix well. Heat the oven to 350 F. Place a piece of wax paper on the counter. Pat meatloaf mixture into a 1-inch-thick rectangle. Place the cooled mushroom filling in the center of the rectangle and flip the other half of the meatloaf mixture over the mushrooms so that the mushrooms are completely enclosed.

Lightly brush a baking pan with cooking spray. Carefully place the meatloaf in the pan or use greaseproof paper to get it into the pan. Bake uncovered for about 47-57 minutes to and then remove from pan. Serve warm.

Polish Black Pudding (Kiszka)

Preparation time: 30 minutes
Cooking time: 2 hours
Nutrition facts (per serving): 68 Calories (Fat 5.03 g, Carbohydrates 3.7 g, Protein 2.31 g)

Ingredients (8 servings)
2 pounds well-marbled pork shoulder
1 pork liver
2 teaspoons salt
7 cups of water
3 cups buckwheat groats
Large, clean pig intestines
2 cups strained pig's blood, mixed with 2 tablespoons vinegar
1 teaspoon pepper
1 teaspoon marjoram

Preparation
Place the pork and pork liver in a large ovenproof pan and cover with water. Add 1 teaspoon of salt and bring to a boil. Reduce heat and simmer until the meat falls off the bones, adding more water if necessary, so that it is always covered. Remove the meat from the pan and reserve the liquid. When the meat has cooled enough to hold, remove the bones, veins, and cartilage and coarsely grind. Put aside.

Scoop the fat from the reserved liquid and add enough water to make 7 cups. Add 1 teaspoon of salt and bring to a boil. Gradually add buckwheat groats, stirring constantly. Bring back to a boil and simmer until the water is absorbed. Heat the oven to 380 F. Cover buckwheat and bake for 32-35 minutes. Have large, clean pig intestines ready. Mix hot buckwheat with reserved ground beef and pork liver. Taste and adjust seasoning. Add pig's blood to which vinegar has been added to keep it from clotting. Add 1 teaspoon of pepper and 1 teaspoon or more of marjoram and mix well.

Fill pork intestines and tie ends with butcher wire or wooden skewers. Place *Kiszka* in a Dutch oven with warm water. Gently bring to a boil, reduce heat and simmer for 38-45 minutes. Remove from the water and serve.

Breaded Chicken Cutlets
(Kotlet Kurczeta)

Preparation time: 20 minutes
Cooking time: 20 minutes
Nutritional Value (per serving): 364 Calories (Fat 23.32 g, Carbs 15.79g, Protein 22.03g)

Ingredients (4 servings)

4 4-ounce boneless chicken breasts
1 egg, beaten with 1 teaspoon of water
8 tablespoons butter, split into 4 pieces
2/3 cup all-purpose flour or as needed for dredging
1 1/2 cups fine breadcrumbs
A few pinches salt and black pepper

Preparation

Remove fat and any gristle from chicken breasts. Pound each to 1/4-inch thickness between two pieces of plastic wrap. Season both sides with salt and pepper. Place 1 piece of butter in the center of each breast and roll like a burrito. The breasts can be placed in the freezer for 35 minutes to ensure that the butter becomes firm again and does not leak out during the cooking process. Dip the breasts in flour, then the egg and then in breadcrumbs. Repeat, double breading the cutlets. Let them dry for 15 minutes before frying them.

Heat 1 inch of oil in a large skillet over 105 F. Slowly fry the cutlets on all sides, about 16-22 minutes in total. Remove from pan, drain on kitchen paper and serve.

Potato, Cabbage and Bacon Casserole

Preparation time: 45 minutes
Cooking time: 45 minutes
Nutrition Facts (per serving): 465 Calories (Fat 31g, Carbohydrates 21 g, Protein 27g)

Ingredients (8 servings)

1 pound bacon, diced
1 large onion, diced
1 cabbage, cored and roughly chopped)
3 large russet potatoes, peeled, cut into 1/2-inch cubes, precooked)
1 teaspoon salt
1 teaspoon pepper
1/2 cup whipped cream
1/2 cup Polish or Swiss cheese, shredded

Preparation

Heat oven to 380 F. In a Dutch oven, fry diced bacon until crisp but not burnt. Use a slotted spoon to remove the bacon and set aside. Some of the bacon fat can be removed if desired, but traditionally it is left in. Add the onion and cabbage to the bacon fat and mix well. Cook for 21-23 minutes or until the cabbage is al dente. Add the well-drained potatoes, 1 teaspoon of salt, 1 teaspoon of pepper, 1/2 cup of cream, and reserved bacon and mix everything. Remove from heat.

Sprinkle the cheese over the cabbage-potato-bacon casserole and cover with foil or lid. Bake for 37 minutes or until the potatoes are almost cooked. Remove the lid and bake for an additional 9-12 minutes or until the cheese has melted and is golden and the potatoes are soft.

Smoked Sausage With Cabbage And Apples

Preparation time: 15 minutes
Cooking time: 2 hours
Nutrition facts (per serving): 466 Calories (Fat 20g, Carbs 59g, Protein 17g)

Ingredients (4 servings)
1/4 cup packed brown sugar
1/2 medium head cabbage, roughly chopped
1 garlic clove, chopped
1 teaspoon salt
1/4 teaspoon nutmeg
1 dash allspice
1 pinch ground black pepper
15 ounces chicken sausage links or another smoked sausage, cut into 1/2-inch pieces
1 cup chopped onion
1 large Granny Smith apple, peeled, cored, roughly chopped
1/4 cup apple juice
3 tablespoons apple cider vinegar

Preparation
Preheat the oven to 330 F. Combine the brown sugar, allspice, garlic, salt, nutmeg and pepper in a bowl. In a large ovenproof casserole dish, place half the cabbage, half the apple, half the onion and half the sausage slices. Sprinkle with half of the brown sugar and spices mixture. Repeat the layers with the remaining cabbage, onion, apple, sausage, and brown sugar mixture. Pour the apple juice and vinegar over the frying pan. Cover and bake for about 2 hours, stirring occasionally. Add more juice if necessary.

Sausage, Cabbage, And Potato Casserole

Preparation time: 20 minutes
Cooking time: 30 minutes
Nutrition Facts (per serving): 559 Calories (Fat 37 g, Protein 18 g, Fiber 3 g)

Ingredients (4 servings)

1 tablespoon of butter
2 large onions, roughly chopped
1 medium head cabbage, roughly chopped or shredded
2 red apples, cored and sliced 1/2-inch thick
2 large potatoes, pre-cooked for 6 minutes, keep the cooking water and roughly chop the potatoes
1 tablespoon herbs
Ground black pepper, to taste
1 tablespoon caraway seeds
1 pound smoked Polish sausage, cut into 6 pieces and scored 3 times diagonally

Preparation

In a large, roasting pan or skillet with a lid, sauté the onion in butter over medium heat until translucent. Without stirring, add the cabbage and sprinkle evenly with the herbs. Add apples, caraway seeds, and pepper without stirring. Top with sausage and 1 cup of potato cooking water. Cover with the lid. When the water starts to boil, reduce the heat and simmer for 12 minutes. Remove the lid and mix all ingredients. Replace the lid and simmer for another 12 minutes. Remove the lid and test if the cabbage is cooked. If there is too much juice, cook over medium heat until reduced.

Hocks With Beer-Honey Glaze (Golonka)

Preparation time: 30 minutes
Cooking time: 3 hours
Nutrition facts (per serving): 456 Calories (Fat 13 g, Protein 17 g, Fiber 15 g)

Ingredients (4 servings)
4 large pork or ham hocks
1 tablespoon salt
1 large onion, peeled and quartered
1 parsnip, peeled
1 rib celery
2 cloves garlic, chopped
1 bay leaf
6 black peppercorns
2 juniper berries, to taste
1 large carrot, peeled
1 tablespoon fresh parsley, chopped
1 teaspoon caraway seeds
1 can of beer
4 tablespoons honey
2 tablespoons of the reserved cooking water

Preparation
Singe the hair from 4 large fresh pork hocks over an open fire. Rinse the hocks and place them in a large Dutch oven or pan with a lid. Add enough water to cover with a few inches. Bring to a boil and remove any foam that comes to the surface.

Add 1 tablespoon of salt, bay leaf, black peppercorns, celery, chopped garlic, juniper berries, the peeled parsnip, carrot, quartered onion, chopped fresh parsley, and caraway seeds, and bring back to a boil. Turn the heat down and simmer, cover, and simmer 2-3 hours or until the meat almost falls off the bones.

Heat the oven to 380 F. Remove the hocks from the pan. Reserve the cooking water for the glaze, while the rest can be the base for a good soup. Transfer hocks to a baking pan that only fits the meat. You want the hocks to almost touch.

In a saucepan, add 1 can of beer, 4 tablespoons of honey and 2 tablespoons of the cooking liquid. Heat until the honey has dissolved. Pour the mixture over the hocks and bake uncovered for 35 to 44 minutes, basting occasionally, until the meat is completely cooked and glazed. Serve with sauerkraut and boiled potatoes.

Beet Leaf Buns Filled With Bread

Preparation time: 30 minutes
Cooking time: 60 minutes
Nutrition facts (per serving): 255 Calories (Fat 16 g, Carbs 21 g, Protein 7 g)

Ingredients (11 servings)

2 1/4 teaspoons active dry yeast
1/4 cup warm water
1/2 teaspoon sugar
1 cup milk, warm
2 cups water, warm
1-ounce butter, melted
4 cups flour, universal
2 large eggs, beaten
1 tablespoon salt
1 tablespoon sugar
3 1/4 cups all-purpose flour
1 tablespoon melted butter
2 bunches beet leaves
3 tablespoons melted butter
1 teaspoon salt
2 tablespoons butter
2 tablespoons flour
1 cup vegetable or meat stock
3/4 cup sour cream
3 tablespoons dill, chopped, fresh
Salt to taste
Pepper to taste

Preparation

Use a fork in a glass measuring cup or small bowl to mix the yeast with 1/4 cup of warm water and 1/2 teaspoon sugar. Let stand for 12 minutes. In a bowl, combine the yeast mixture, milk, 2 cups of warm water, 1 ounce of melted butter. Add 4 cups of flour and mix until well combined. Cover with greased plastic wrap and let rise in a warm place for 50-60 minutes or until doubled in size.

Punch down the dough and transfer it to a stand mixer with a dough hook; add beaten eggs, 1 tablespoon of sugar, 1 tablespoon of salt and 3 1/4 cups of flour. Knead until the dough is smooth. Coat the top with melted butter or oil, cover with plastic wrap, and let rise for 90-120 minutes or until doubled.

Meanwhile, wash the beet leaves and blanch them in boiling water for 30 seconds or until they are pliable. Remove from the water and add cold water to stop the boiling process. Drain.

When the dough has doubled, knock it down. Take a walnut-sized piece of dough, extend it into a rectangular shape and place it on a beet leaf. Roll up loosely, as with cabbage rolls, but leave the sides open so that the dough can expand as it rises and then bakes. If you like bigger buns, use more bread dough, but remember it will grow.

Line the bottom and sides of a Dutch oven or other large pans with beet leaves. Put a layer of beet buns on the bottom. Brush with melted butter or other fat and salt. Repeat the layering, finish with melted butter or fat, and salt on top. Cover with plastic wrap and let rise for 2 hours or until doubled.

Heat the oven to 350 F. When the rolls have risen, remove the plastic wrap and cover with a layer of beet leaves. Cover with a tight-fitting lid after you brushed the inside of the lid with butter or fat. Bake for 1 hour and serve hot with creamy dill sauce.

While the rolls are baking, make the sauce by melting 2 tablespoons of butter in a small saucepan. Stir in 2 tablespoons of flour and cook until the mixture is bubbling. Add stock and, while whisking constantly, bring to a slow boil. Cook until thick and beat regularly. Place sour cream in a heatproof bowl and temper by whipping 2 small spoons of the stock mixture, then add tempered sour cream to the sauce and stir until smooth. Add 3 tablespoons of chopped fresh dill and adjust the seasoning. Keep warm until ready to serve.

Hunter's Stew

Preparation time: 30 minutes
Cooking time: 30 minutes
Nutrition Facts (per serving): 148 Calories (Carbs 5g, Fat 14g, Protein 21g)

Ingredients (12 servings)
1 1/2 cups bacon, chopped
1 1/2 pounds boneless pork, cubed
6 cloves garlic, finely chopped
5 onions, quartered
1 pound mushrooms, cleaned and quartered
4 beef stock cubes in 1 cup of hot water
4 cups canned tomatoes, chopped, with juice
3 tablespoons sugar
4 bay leaves
5 cups good quality sauerkraut
5 apples, peeled, cored, and chopped
2 cups ham, cubed
2 1/2 cups smoked Polish or similar sausage, diced
1/2 to 1 pound leftover beef or veal, cubed
1/2 to 1 pound leftover chicken breast, cubed
Salt and pepper to taste

Preparation
Fry the bacon in a frying pan to release its fat, then mix in the pieces of pork, garlic, onions, and mushrooms. Sauté for 6-8 minutes or until the meat is browned.

Pour in the beef stock cubes and hot water, tomatoes with their juice, sugar, bay leaves, sauerkraut, and apples or applesauce and bring to a boil. Reduce heat and simmer, covered, for about 2 hours. Stir in ham, sausage, remaining beef or veal, and chicken, cover, and cook over medium heat for 27-33 minutes more. Adjust herbs.

When ready to serve, remove the bay leaves and taste for seasoning. Ladle into bowls and serve with boiled potatoes, a bowl of sour cream, and thick, crispy rye bread.

Slow Cooker Kielbasa

Preparation time: 10 minutes
Cooking time: 7 hours
Nutrition facts (per serving): 486 Calories (Fat 22 g, Carbohydrates 62 g, Protein 13 g)

Ingredients (4 servings)
1 pound sauerkraut
1/2 cup brown sugar, packed
3/4 teaspoon salt
1/8 teaspoon pepper
1 pound kielbasa or another similar smoked sausage
4 apples, sharp, thickly sliced
1/2 teaspoon caraway seeds
3/4 cup apple juice

Preparation
Rinse the sauerkraut and press it dry to remove the brine. Put half of the sauerkraut in the slow cooker. Cut the sausage into 2-inch pieces. Place the sausage pieces in the slow cooker. Keep putting the ingredients in the slow cooker in this order: the sliced apples, brown sugar, salt, pepper, and caraway seeds. Finish with the remaining sauerkraut. Pour the apple juice over it. Cover and cook on low for 7-9 hours or until apples are tender. Stir before serving.

Crockpot Kielbasa With Cabbage And Potatoes

Preparation time: 8 minutes
Cooking time: 8 hours
Nutrition facts (per serving): 403 Calories (Fat 25g, Carbs 28g, Protein 18g)

Ingredients (6 servings)

1/2 cup cabbage, roughly chopped
2 pounds kielbasa or similar smoked sausage, cut into 1-inch pieces
1 1/2 cups chicken stock
1 medium potato, diced
1 large onion, halved and thinly sliced
1 teaspoon salt
1/2 teaspoon caraway seeds

Preparation

Cut the potato, cabbage and onion into pieces and add them in the slow cooker. Add the sliced kielbasa along with the stock, salt, and caraway and mix everything. Cover and cook on low for 8 hours, or high for 4 hours, before serving.

Boiled Potatoes With Onion And Dill

Preparation time: 15 minutes
Cooking time: 45 minutes
Nutrition facts (per serving): 136 Calories (Fat 7 g, Carbohydrates 18 g, Protein 2 g)

Ingredients (6 servings)

1 tablespoon sugar
6 large red potatoes, peeled and cut into medium-sized pieces
1 teaspoon salt
2 tablespoons olive oil
1 tablespoon butter
1 1/2 cups onions, chopped
2 tablespoons fresh dill, finely chopped

Preparation

Heat the olive oil with the butter in a medium skillet until the butter just begins to foam. Add onions and cook over low heat for 12 minutes or until they start to brown. Stir frequently.

Reduce heat and continue cooking for 10 minutes, stirring occasionally, until onions turn golden brown. Sprinkle with sugar, if desired, and cook for another minute or two, stirring to incorporate. Put aside.

Boil potatoes in a large pan with salted water for 12 to 16 minutes. Drain well, put them back in the pan, and warm them on low heat for a few minutes to evaporate the remaining water. Remove from heat. Add caramelized onions, salt, and dill. Toss until all ingredients are well incorporated. Place the potatoes on a serving dish and serve warm.

Gdansk Casserole

Preparation time: 15 minutes
Cooking time: 50 minutes
Nutrition facts (per serving): 534 Calories (Fat 29 g, Carbs 47 g, Protein 22 g)

Ingredients (6 servings)

1 pound sauerkraut, rinsed, drained, and pressed dry
4 ounces uncooked *kluski* noodles
1 (14-ounce) package smoked kielbasa, sliced 1/4 inch thick
1 can (10.75 ounces) cream of mushroom soup
1/4 cup caramelized onion
1 1/2 teaspoons yellow mustard
4 ounces grated Swiss cheese
1/4 cup breadcrumbs

Preparation

Heat oven to 355 F. Lightly brushes a large glass or ceramic loaf pan or frying pan with cooking spray. Mix soup, caramelized onion, and mustard and set aside. Layer half of the sauerkraut in the prepared pan. Put half of the *kluski* on top, followed by half of the kielbasa. Divide half of the soup mixture over the kielbasa. Repeat the layers with the remaining ingredients. Sprinkle the grated cheese evenly over the top. Top with breadcrumbs. Place the casserole on a baking sheet to catch any dripping. Bake for 55 minutes or until golden and bubbly. Give the pan half a turn after it has been baking 30 minutes. Serve.

Polish Meatballs in Sour Cream (Klopsiki)

Preparation time: 20 minutes
Cooking time: 30 minutes
Nutrition Facts (per serving): 582 Calories (Fat 23 g, Protein 54 g, Fiber 20 g)

Ingredients (5 servings)
Meatballs
1 slice stale white bread
1/2 cup milk
3/4 pound ground beef, chuck
1/2 pound ground pork, lean
1 onion, finely chopped
1 egg, lightly beaten
Salt and black pepper to taste
2 tablespoons breadcrumbs
2 tablespoons beef stock

Gravy
Pan juices
3/4 cup sour cream
2 tablespoons all-purpose flour
1 1/2 cups of water

Mushroom sauce
2 ounces dried Polish or porcini mushrooms
2 cups boiling water
2 tablespoons butter

1 large onion, roughly chopped

8 ounces mushrooms

1 cup sour cream

2 tablespoons all-purpose flour

1 teaspoon beef or chicken base

Salt and pepper to taste

Preparation

In a large bowl, soak the bread in milk until soft. Add egg, salt, beef, pork, onion and pepper to taste and mix well. If the mixture feels too mushy, add 2 tablespoons of breadcrumbs. To make sure your seasonings are good, bake a small patty, taste it, and adjust as needed. Heat oven to 330 F. Use a medium cookie scoop to measure the meatballs, form the meatballs and give it a final roll with damp hands. Lightly brush a skillet with cooking spray and brown meatballs on all sides. Transfer to a baking pan, add 2 tablespoons beef stock or water and cook, uncovered, for 32-34 minutes.

Gather the gravy ingredients. Remove the fat from the surface of the pan juices and add 3/4 cup of sour cream mixed with 2 tablespoons of flour. Add 1 1/2 cups of boiling water and beat until smooth. Cook until thick. Serve with meatballs and your preferred starch.

To make the mushroom sauce, place dried mushrooms in a heatproof bowl and pour 2 cups of boiling water over it. Let it steep for 32-34 minutes. Meanwhile, in a medium saucepan, fry 1 large chopped onion in butter until caramelized. If you are using fresh mushrooms, put them in the pan once the onions are translucent. Otherwise, place un-drained canned mushrooms in the pan once the onions are completely caramelized. Using your fingers, remove the dried mushrooms from the soaking liquid and put them in the pan with onions. Carefully add the soaking liquid to the pan, taking care not to disturb the sediment on the bottom.

Add beef or chicken base, salt, and pepper. Bring to a boil, reduce heat and simmer, covered, for 31-33 minutes. In a medium bowl, combine 2 tablespoons of flour to 1 cup of sour cream. Temper the sour cream by adding 3 tablespoons of hot mushroom liquid, 1 tablespoon at a time, and whipping until smooth. Slowly pour the tempered sour cream back into the mushroom sauce, whisking constantly. Simmer for 6 to 11 minutes or until thickened. Serve.

Mushroom Pierogi
With Naleśniki Filling

Preparation time: 10 minutes
Cooking time: 15 minutes
Nutrition Facts (per serving): 261 Calories (Fat 16 g, Carbs 21 g, Protein 10 g)

Ingredients (5 servings)
Mushroom Stuffing
3 cups mushrooms, fresh, finely chopped
2 onions, finely chopped
4 tablespoons butter
4 tablespoons breadcrumbs, fine dry
Salt and pepper, to taste

Pierogi dough
1 teaspoon of salt
3/4 cup chicken stock
4 cups flour
2 large eggs
5 tablespoons sour cream
3 tablespoons oil

Preparation
In a large frying pan, fry the mushrooms and onions in butter. Remove from heat and let cool. Add breadcrumbs, salt, and pepper and mix well. Use immediately.

In a large bowl, combine the eggs, sour cream, oil, salt, and chicken stock until well blended. Add flour and knead by hand or in a stand mixer until dough is smooth. Wrap in plastic and let rest for at least 15 minutes, before serving.

Noodles With Poppy Seeds
(Kluski Z Makiem)

Preparation time: 10 minutes
Cooking time: 20 minutes
Nutrition facts (per serving): 455 Calories (Fiber 24g, Protein 59g, Fat 12g)

Ingredients (6 servings)

3 cups egg noodles, cooked and kept warm
2 tablespoons butter
1/2 cup raisins
1/2 pound poppy seeds
1 1/2 cups milk
1/2 to 1 cup honey
1/2 cup almonds, chopped
1 tablespoon candied orange zest, chopped

Preparation

Bring poppy seeds and milk to a boil in a large saucepan. Cover and let stand for 11-13 hours. Put poppy seeds in a sieve to drain any moisture. Grind the poppy seeds twice. Mix ground poppy seeds with raisins, honey, nuts and orange zest, if using. Put in a saucepan and heat through. Combine warm egg noodles with 2 tablespoons of butter and poppy seed mixture. Serve warm.

Polish Sausages And Sauerkraut With Apples

Preparation time: 15 minutes
Cooking time: 6 hours
Nutrition Facts (per serving): 934 Calories (Total fat 0.9g, Protein 0.8g, Sugar 3.6g)

Ingredients (4 servings)

16 ounces of sauerkraut
1 pound of kielbasa or smoked sausage
3 apples, peeled, cored and sliced
1/2 cup packed brown sugar
3/4 teaspoon salt
1/8 teaspoon pepper
1/2 teaspoon caraway seeds
2/3 cup apple juice or apple cider

Preparation

Rinse sauerkraut, drain and squeeze out any brine. Put half the sauerkraut in a slow cooker. Cut sausage into 2-inch pieces. Place in a slow cooker. Keep layers in the slow cooker, apples, brown sugar, salt, and pepper. Sprinkle with caraway seeds, if using. Top with the remaining sauerkraut. Add apple juice. Do not stir the mixture before cooking. Cover and cook for 3 - 4 hours on high or 7 hours on low, or until apples are tender. Stir before serving.

Gdansk Smoked Sausage
And Sauerkraut

Preparation time: 15 minutes
Cooking time: 60 minutes
Nutrition Facts (per serving): 769 Calories (Fat 56 g, Carbohydrates 29 g, Protein 37 g)

Ingredients (7 servings)
1 pound bacon, cut into 1/2-inch pieces and fried
2 pounds sauerkraut, rinsed and pressed
2 pounds Polish sausage, smoked; cut into 1.5-inch pieces
1 cup apple juice
1/4 cup brown sugar, packed, more or less to taste
2 Granny Smith apples, peeled, cored, and sliced 1/2 inch thick)
1 tablespoon caraway seeds

Preparation
Grease a baking tin lightly with cooking spray. Heat the oven to 330 F. In a large bowl, combine sauerkraut, smoked sausage, bacon, apple juice, brown sugar, apples, and caraway seeds. Transfer to the prepared baking dish. Cover and bake for 55-60 minutes. Stir after 30 minutes, adding more apple juice if necessary. Cool and refrigerate overnight. Transfer it to a slow cooker the next day. Heat over medium heat, stirring occasionally, until ready to serve.

Roast Duck With Apples

Preparation time: 20 minutes
Cooking time: 2 hours
Nutrition facts (per serving): 347 Calories (Fat 18 g, Protein 67 g, Fiber 12 g)

Ingredients (3 servings)
4 1/2 pounds duck
2 medium apples, washed, peeled, cored and chopped
2 tablespoons fresh marjoram, finely chopped
3 garlic cloves, crushed
Salt and black pepper
2 1/4 pounds of potatoes
1 tablespoon caraway seeds

Preparation
Preheat the oven to 480 F. Rinse the duck with water and pat dry. Fill the cavity with the pieces of apple. Rub the skin well with the marjoram, garlic, salt, and pepper. Place on a large plate, cover, and marinate for 45 minutes. Place the duck in a roasting tin. Collect the marinade left in the plate and add a little more water to make 1 cup of liquid. Pour this liquid around the duck in the roasting pan, not over it; otherwise, you will wash the marinade off.

Roast the duck uncovered for 12 minutes, then reduce heat to 325 F and roast for 2 hours. About every half an hour, use a fine skewer to poke holes in the duck's skin to allow the juices to escape and then baste the duck with the moisture that collects at the bottom of the pan.

Wash the potatoes and cut them in halves or quarters. When the duck has been in the oven for about 1 hour, salt the potatoes, put them in the roasting pan with the duck and sprinkle with caraway seeds. Next time you baste the duck, turn the potatoes over and make sure they are well coated with the duck juice. Add a pinch of caraway seeds.

Polish Crab-Filled Salmon Pin Wheels

Preparation time: 20 minutes
Cooking time: 20 minutes
Nutrition Facts (per serving): 671 Calories (Fat 39 g, Carbs 12 g, Protein 62 g)

Ingredients (4 servings)
Crab filling
2 tablespoons butter
1/4 cup onions, finely chopped
1/4 cup celery, finely chopped
1 teaspoon lemon juice
1 cup crabmeat, diced, cooked
1/2 cup soft breadcrumbs
1 large egg, beaten
1/2 teaspoon dried dill or 2 teaspoons chopped fresh dill

Salmon
2 pounds salmon, bones removed
Salt and black pepper to taste
1/4 cup of dry white wine
2 tablespoons butter, melted

Preparation
In a medium skillet, fry the celery and onion in butter until translucent. Remove from heat, cool, and transfer to a medium bowl. Add lemon juice, crabmeat, breadcrumbs, egg, and dill and mix well.

Prepare the salmon. Cut the salmon in half lengthwise into two pieces. Season both sides with salt and pepper. Divide the crab filling over each piece of salmon. If you have leftover filling, use it to make crab cakes or stuff into mushrooms. Roll the salmon up into cylinders at the wide end. Cover with plastic wrap and refrigerate for about an hour to make cutting easier.

Heat the oven to 400 F. With a sharp knife, cut the salmon into 2-inch portions. Lightly brush a glass baking dish with cooking spray. Place pinwheels in the pan with the cutting edge down and pour the wine around it. Brush pinwheels with butter, cover loosely with foil and bake for 17 to 22 minutes. Serve.

Crock-Pot Sweet And Sour Kielbasa

Preparation time: 10 minutes
Cooking time: 2 hours
Nutrition facts (per serving): 324 Calories (Protein 42g, Fat 15g, Fiber 8g)

Ingredients (4 servings)

1 pound kielbasa
1 (10 ounces) jar of red currant jelly
4 tablespoons spicy mustard

Preparation

Cut the kielbasa into bite-sized pieces. Put the kielbasa in a saucepan and cover with water. Place the pan on medium-high heat, bring it to a boil and cook for 12 minutes. Combine the berry jelly and mustard in the slow cooker. Add kielbasa to the slow cooker mixture and stir well. Cover and cook on low for 2 hours. Serve.

Crock Pot Easiest Chops

Preparation time: 5 minutes
Cooking time: 7 hours
Nutrition facts (per serving): 416 Calories (Fat 23 g, Carbs 4 g, Protein 45 g)

Ingredients
4 pork chops, trimmed well to exclude excess fat
1 envelope onion soup mix
1 (10-ounce) can chicken stock

Preparation
Brown the pork chops in a nonstick skillet over medium-high heat for about 3 minutes on each side. Place the pork chops in a 4-quart crockpot. Combine the soup mix and the chicken stock in a medium bowl and stir into a mixture. Pour this mixture over the pork chops in the slow cooker.

Cover the slow cooker and cook the pork chops over 200 F for 8 hours. When done, the pork should register at least 145 F on a meat thermometer, but chances are they will be well cooked. The chops can fall apart because they are so tender.

Thicken the liquid for gravy if you wish. Pour about 2 cups of liquid into a medium saucepan and add 2 tablespoons of cornstarch mixed with 1/3 cup of water. Bring to a boil and cook until thicker. Adjust the seasoning to taste, before serving.

Polish Hamburgers (Mielone Kotlety)

Preparation time: 20 minutes
Cooking time: 30 minutes
Nutrition facts (per serving): 241 Calories (Fat 11 g, Carbohydrates 6 g, Protein 26 g)

Ingredients (6 servings)
1 slice stale white bread
1/2 cup milk
3/4 pound ground beef
1/2 pound pork, lean ground
1 small onion, finely chopped
1 egg, lightly beaten
Salt and pepper, to taste

Preparation
In a large bowl, soak the bread in milk until soft. Add beef, pork, onion, egg, salt, and pepper and mix well. If the mixture feels too mushy, add 2 tablespoons of breadcrumbs. Divide the meat mixture into 6 portions and shape each into a round burger shape. Lightly brush a frying pan with cooking spray and fry the patties slowly over low heat until golden brown on both sides. Serve.

Polish Sauerkraut Pierogi

Preparation time: 5 minutes
Cooking time: 10 minutes
Nutrition Facts (per serving): 441 Calories (Fat 36 g, Carbohydrates 23 g, Protein 9 g)

Ingredients (6 servings)
Sauerkraut filling
2 tablespoons of cooking oil
1 large onion, finely chopped
1 pound sauerkraut, drained, rinsed, and chopped
2 large carrots, peeled and grated
1 teaspoon salt
1/2 teaspoon black pepper
2 tablespoons sour cream

Pierogi dough
2 eggs
5 tablespoons sour cream
3 tablespoons vegetable oil
1 teaspoon salt
3/4 cup chicken stock
4 cups flour
4 ounces butter
1 cup onion, finely chopped

Preparation
Heat 2 tablespoons of oil in a large skillet on medium-high heat. Add the onions and cook until tender but not brown. Add sauerkraut and carrots. Cook, stirring

often, for 12 to 16 minutes or until the volume has decreased and the sauerkraut is tender. Remove from heat and stir in 1 teaspoon of salt, pepper, and 2 tablespoons of sour cream. If the mixture doesn't hold its shape when squeezed together, add more sour cream. Let filling cool completely before filling the pierogi dough. If desired, keep covered in the refrigerator for a day before use.

In a large bowl, combine 3 tablespoons oil, eggs, 5 tablespoons sour cream, 1 teaspoon salt, and chicken stock until well blended. Add flour and knead until the dough is smooth. Wrap in plastic and let rest for at least 15 minutes before rolling. Remove the sauerkraut filling from the refrigerator and let it come to room temperature. On a lightly floured work surface, roll the dough out to 1/8 inch thickness. Cut the dough with a 3-inch round cutter. Gather leftovers, cover with plastic wrap, and set aside.

Use a tablespoon to spread the sauerkraut filling on all of the dough circles before folding them. With clean, dry hands, fold the dough over the filling to create a half-moon shape. Press the edges together with your fingers or fork like a pie. Roll, cut, and fill the remaining pieces of dough.

Bring a deep saucepan of salted water to a boil. Drop 11 pierogi at a time into the water. Stir once so that they don't stick to the bottom. When they come to the surface, cook for 4 minutes or until dough is cooked.

Remove with a slotted spoon from the pan onto a lightly oiled baking sheet. Pierogi will stick together if drained in a colander, even if the colander is covered with cooking spray. Repeat until all the pierogi are cooked. Serve as is with melted butter or fry in butter.

Add butter and 1 cup of chopped onion to a heavy, large skillet and sauté until the onion is translucent. Add pierogi and cook until golden brown on both sides and onion is cooked through. Serve warm.

APPETIZERS AND DIPS

Homemade Bread Bowl

Preparation time: 5 minutes
Cooking time: 35 minutes
Nutrition facts (per serving): 286 Calories (Fat 1g, Sodium 396mg, Fiber 2g, Protein 10g)

Ingredients (1 serving)
3 cups flour
1 1/4 cups lukewarm water
2 tablespoons olive oil, divided
1 teaspoon active dry yeast
2 teaspoons salt

Preparation
Add water, flour, yeast, salt, and a tablespoon of olive oil to a bowl and stir until it becomes a rough dough. Use your hands to blend the dough into a smooth dough. Place the dough in an oiled bowl and let rise, covered, for an hour. If you are making smaller rolls, divide the dough into four balls. If you aren't, you can use the frying pan method below to make the bowl.

Preheat the oven to 480 F. Place a medium roasting pan in the oven to heat for 18 minutes. Shape the dough into a single, tight ball and place it on a piece of parchment paper. Transfer it to the hot frying pan and bake, covered, for 33 minutes.

After 33 minutes, remove the lid from the pan and bake the bread uncovered for an additional 14 minutes or until browned. Let the bread cool for 15 minutes. Then cut a lid off the top of the bread and set aside.

Dig out the inside of the bread to remove most of the soft bread. Cut the top of the bread cover into cubes. Brush the inside of the bread bowl with the remaining olive oil and bake for another 12 minutes to toast the inside of the bread bowl. Serve.

Air Fryer Ranch Kale Chips

Preparation time: 2 minutes
Cooking time: 12 minutes
Nutrition facts (per serving): 150 Calories (Carbohydrates 3 g, Fat 15 g)

Ingredients

10 kale leaves
1 teaspoon garlic powder
1 teaspoon onion powder
1 teaspoon dried dill
2 tablespoons olive oil
1 tablespoon nutritional yeast flakes
1 teaspoon salt

Preparation

Remove the curled leaves from the hard stalk of the kale. Break the leaves into smaller, bite-sized pieces. Beat the olive oil, nutritional yeast flakes, garlic powder, onion powder, dried dill, and salt in a large bowl. Add the pieces of kale to the bowl and toss. Make sure to evenly cover the leaves with the herbs. Add the kale to the air fryer basket. Set the air fryer to 410 F and cook for 12 minutes, shaking halfway through the cooking time. Serve.

Kielbasa Appetizer
With Apple Jelly

Preparation time: 5 minutes
Cooking time: 2 hours
Nutrition Facts (per serving): 230 Calories (Fat 19 g, Carbohydrates 9 g, Protein 8 g)

Ingredients (15 servings)
2 pounds kielbasa
1 (18 ounces) jar of apple jelly
1 (9 ounces) jar of prepared mustard

Preparation
Cut kielbasa 1/2-inch thick. Mix jelly and mustard in a slow cooker or crockpot. Add sliced kielbasa and mix until the meat is coated. Set the slow cooker on low to cook for 2 hours. Stir every 25-35 minutes. Serve.

Raw Polish Carrot Surowka

Preparation time: 20 minutes
Nutrition facts (per serving): 178 calories (Fat 1 g, Carbohydrates 18g, Protein 1g)

Ingredients (6 servings)

5 large carrots, peeled and coarsely grated
1 Granny Smith apple, peeled, cored and coarsely grated
1 tablespoon lemon juice
1 tablespoon sunflower oil
1/2 cup dark or light raisins, soaked in water for 15 minutes)
Salt and sugar to taste

Preparation

In a bowl, combine apple, lemon juice, carrots, sunflower or vegetable oil, drained raisins, salt to taste, and sugar to taste. After the ingredients are thoroughly mixed, cover and refrigerate until cold. Serve chilled.

Polish Pork Lard Spread (Smalec)

Preparation time: 20 minutes
Cooking time: 30 minutes
Nutrition Facts (per serving): 499 Calories (Fat 29g, Carbs 12g, Protein 46g)

Ingredients (2 servings)
2 1/4 pounds white pork fat or diced leaf lard
2 onions, finely chopped
4 cloves garlic, finely chopped
1/2 pound fat bacon, diced
2 large sour apples, peeled, cored and cut into small cubes
1/8 teaspoon pepper
1 teaspoon salt
1 teaspoon marjoram

Preparation
Grind the diced white pork fat and put it in a large skillet. Sauté until fat is transparent, stirring occasionally. Add the onion, garlic, and bacon and fry until the bacon is golden brown, and it released it fat. Add the apples and season with any marjoram, pepper, and salt to taste. Do not add to much salt since the bacon is probably quite salty. But you have to add enough to make the Smalec taste good.

Transfer to a stoneware jar or heat resistant jar. Leave at room temperature until the fat has solidified. Serve this spread on rye bread topped with pickles.

Polish Pork-And-Beef Pate (Pasztet)

Preparation time: 100 minutes
Cooking time: 15 minutes
Nutrition facts (per serving): 332 Calories (Fat 23 g, Carbohydrates 7g, Protein 23g)

Ingredients (20 servings)

2.2 pounds beef, flank steak
1 pound of pork, boneless shoulder
11 ounces of pork fat
1 bay leaf
4 allspice berries
5 black peppercorns
2 bread rolls, dry
2 onions, peeled and thinly sliced
2 tablespoons of vegetable oil
2 teaspoons salt
1/4 teaspoon black pepper
1 pinch nutmeg
3 cloves garlic, crushed
1 tablespoon vegetable oil
1 tablespoon breadcrumbs

Preparation

Wash the beef, pork, and pork fat. Drain and transfer to a large saucepan. Add bay leaf, allspice, black peppercorns, and pour in enough cold water to cover the meat. Simmer until the meat is cooked. Remove the pan from the heat. Place the buns on top of the stock to soak them. Sauté the peeled and thinly sliced onions in a little oil in a frying pan.

When the meat has cooled, remove it from the stock. Grind the meat together with the roll and the fried onions twice in a meat grinder to a smooth consistency. Season with pepper, nutmeg, salt and crushed garlic. Mix these ingredients well. The pâté mixture should be moist. If it is too dry, add some meat stock.

Grease a mold or baking pan with oil and sprinkle with breadcrumbs. Transfer the pate mixture to the pan and fill it 3/4 full. Bake for about 45 minutes in an oven heated to 345 F. Allow to cool before removing, slicing and serving.

Zapiekanka

Preparation time: 15 minutes
Cooking time: 15 minutes
Nutrition Facts (per serving): 249 Calories (Fat 25g, Carbs 35g,
 Protein 20g)

Ingredients (4 servings)

1 long French loaf, cut in half and then cut in half horizontally to make 4 pieces
Thinly sliced ham, to taste
2 cups mushrooms, baked
Raw or cooked vegetables, to taste
Mayonnaise, to taste
3 cups grated processed cheese

Preparation

If the bread is long, cut it into 3 pieces and halve each horizontally, otherwise cut it into 2 pieces. Place ham or similar meat, baked mushrooms, vegetables of your choice and cheese on each slice of bread and toast in a hot oven until the bread is crispy and the cheese has melted. Drizzle with mayonnaise and serve warm.

Pickle Herring For Polish Rollmops (Rolmopsy)

Preparation time: 60 minutes
Nutritional facts (per serving): 192 Calories (Fat 7 g, Carbohydrates 8g, Protein 1g)

Ingredients (18 servings)
4 salty herrings
2 tablespoons of black pepper
1 cup of water
1 bay leaf
3 tablespoons of oil
2 tablespoons Polish granular mustard
1 large onion, finely chopped
2 medium pickles, quartered
1/2 cup white vinegar
Pinch of sugar

Preparation
Remove the heads from the fish. Let it soak in a large pot of cold water for about 24 hours and change the water two to three times. Make sure there are no scales on the fish to clean. Cut open the abdomen and remove the intestines. Remove the spleen from male herring and set aside. Remove and discard the roe from female herring. Wash the herring pits well. Remove the bones.

Eight fillets should be ready. Spread each with some pepper, mustard, and onion. Place a piece of pickle on the small end of the fillet and roll it up, securing it with a toothpick. Place in a clean, sterilized jar. Continue with the remaining fillets.

In a small saucepan, bring water, vinegar, bay leaf, and remaining sliced onion to a boil. Cool to lukewarm. Add oil and sugar and mix well. Adjust herbs if necessary. Pour lukewarm pickling liquid over the herring. Cover the jar and put it in the refrigerator for three to five days, after which the herring is ready to eat. It can be refrigerated for up to 8 days.

Cottage Cheese Dip Gzik

Preparation time: 5 minutes
Cooking time: 5 minutes
Nutrition Facts (per serving): 345 Calories (Fat 20g, Protein 15g, Carbs 20g)

Ingredients (1 serving)
1 cup cottage cheese
6 radishes
1 bunch of chives (1/2 cup finely chopped)
1 heaped tablespoon of Greek yogurt
Salt pepper

Preparation
Add cottage cheese to a bowl. Finely chop the radishes and chives and add to the cottage cheese. Add Greek yogurt. Season with salt and pepper. Mix everything with the fork. Serve on bread or with boiled potatoes.

Salmon Spread
(Pasta Rybna Tososiowa)

Preparation time: 10 minutes
Nutrition facts (per servings): 216 Calories (Fat 4g, Carbohydrates 8 g, Protein 12 g)

Ingredients (1 serving)

7 ounces piece salmon

2 cloves garlic

2 tablespoons ketchup

1 teaspoon chopped onion

1 teaspoon butter

4 ounces cream cheese

1 teaspoon fresh dill

Preparation

Sprinkle the raw fish with salt and pepper and fry in butter for 8-11 minutes or until done. Remove the cooked fish from the pan and let it cool. Once the fish is cold, put it in a blender or food processor with ketchup, cream cheese, and garlic and blend into a smooth paste. Remove from blender to a bowl and add the finely chopped onion and dill. Mix with a spoon or spatula. Add salt and pepper to taste and refrigerate before serving.

Gdansk Smoked Salmon Dip

Preparation time: 10 minutes
Nutrition Facts (per serving): 90 Calories (Fat 7g, Carbohydrates 4g, Protein 2g)

Ingredients (2 servings)
8 ounces cream cheese, softened at room temperature
1/2 cup sour cream
2 lemons
1/8 teaspoon black pepper
8 ounces smoked salmon, finely chopped
3 tablespoons chopped chives, plus more for garnish
1 tablespoon Dijon mustard
2 tablespoons small capers
1/2 teaspoon pepper

Preparation
In the bowl of a stand mixer, beat the cream cheese and sour cream with the paddle attachment on medium speed until smooth. With the mixer on low, add the chives, mustard, capers, zest, and juice of 1 lemon and black pepper. Mix until all ingredients are incorporated. Transfer to a bowl and whisk the mixture into a smooth mixture.

Fold in the salmon and pepper, if using, by hand. Taste and add the juice of the remaining lemon, 1 teaspoon at a time, if you think it is necessary. Serve immediately or refrigerate until serving.

Fish Paste With Chili

Preparation time: 10 minutes
Cooking time: 10 minutes
Nutrition facts (per serving): 149 calories (carbohydrates 0%, Fat 1g, Protein 2g)

Ingredients (2 servings)

6 ounces smoked mackerel
1 pinch chili
2 tablespoons olive oil
3 ounces cream cheese
2 teaspoons lemon juice
2 tablespoons tablespoon horseradish

Preparation

Carefully peel the skin from the mackerel and remove the bones. Put all ingredients in a blender and mix briefly until well blended. Serve.

Polish Garlic Sauce

Preparation time: 15 minutes
Cooking time: 15 minutes
Nutrition facts (per serving): 567 Calories (Fat 60 g, Carbs 5.3 g)

Ingredients (1 serving)
4 garlic cloves, finely chopped
1/2 cup yogurt
1/2 cup mayonnaise
1/2 teaspoon salt
1/4 teaspoon pepper
1 teaspoon parsley or thyme chopped, fresh or dried

Preparation
Combine all ingredients; allow to rest for 13-15 minutes to allow the flavors to merge before serving. Mix well and serve.

Bohemian Kolaches

Preparation time: 30 minutes
Cooking time: 10 minutes
Nutrition facts (per serving): 164 Calories (Fat 3 g, Fiber 1 g, Protein 4 g)

Ingredients (3 servings)
2 packages (1/4 ounce each) active dry yeast
1/2 cup sugar, divided
2 cups warm milk
6 1/2 cups all-purpose flour
4 egg yolks, room temperature
1 teaspoon salt
1/4 cup butter, softened
2 cups canned plums, poppy seed, cherry filling
1 egg white, beaten

Preparation
In a bowl, dissolve yeast and 1 tablespoon of sugar in warm milk. Let alone for 12 minutes. In another bowl, combine 2 cups of flour, remaining sugar, egg yolks, salt, butter, and yeast/milk mixture. Mix until smooth. Add enough leftover flour to make a stiff dough.

Place the dough on a floured surface and knead for 7-10 minutes into a smooth and elastic dough. Add extra flour if necessary. Place dough in a greased bowl and turn once to grease the top. Cover, let rise in a warm place until doubled in bulk, about 55-65 minutes.

Punch the dough down and let it rise again. Roll out on a floured surface to 1/2-inch thickness. Cut with a tall glass or 2 ½-inch cutter. Place them on greased baking trays; let rise until doubled, about 43-46 minutes.

Press firmly in the center of each cake to make a hollow. Fill each cake with a heaped tablespoon of filling of your choice. Brush the dough with egg white. Bake at 355 F for 12-14 minutes or until the buns are lightly golden brown. Serve.

DESSERTS

Polish Filled Cookies (Kolacziki)

Preparation time: 30 minutes
Nutrition facts (per serving): 130 Calories (Fat 7 g, Carbohydrates 16 g, Protein 2 g)

Ingredients (3 servings)
1/4 cup sour cream, room temperature
1 (2 1/4 teaspoons) package of active dry yeast
1 cup (2 sticks) unsalted butter, cut into small pieces
2 cups all-purpose flour, plus more for dusting
1 cup of canned fruit
1 large egg, beaten

Preparation
Preheat the oven to 400 F. Combine sour cream and yeast in a small bowl. Set aside 12-14 minutes or until slightly bubbly. Stir in the egg with a wooden spoon until smooth. Put aside. Use two knives or a pastry cutter to cut butter into the flour until it resembles a coarse meal. Stir in the sour cream mixture with a spoon until the dough comes together.

On a lightly floured surface, roll out the dough to 1/4 inch thick. Cut into 2 1/2-inch rounds. Transfer to ungreased baking sheets, about 1 1/2 inches apart. Cover with a clean tea towel or plastic wrap. Let sit for 17 minutes. Make a fingerprint in the center of each cookie. Fill each fingerprint with 1 teaspoon of jam. Bake for 13-16 minutes or until the edges are golden. Place the pans in the rack to cool. Let cookies cool on pans for 7 minutes. Remove cookies to a plate. Dust with icing.

Poppy Seed Bun (Makowiec)

Preparation time: 2 hours
Cooking time: 60 minutes
Nutrition facts (per serving): 290 Calories (Fat 23g, Fiber 12g, Protein 41g)

Ingredients (16 servings)
Dough
1 packet of yeast, active dry
2 cups warm milk warm
8 cups flour
3/4 cup sugar
1 teaspoon salt
5 eggs
4 ounces butter, melted

Poppyseed filling
1 pound poppy seeds, ground
1 cup of sugar
6 ounces butter, softened
1 cup warm milk
1 tablespoon lemon zest

Preparation
Grind the poppy seeds in a coffee, seed or spice grinder. In a medium bowl, combine lemon zest, 1 cup sugar, 6 ounces butter and 1 cup hot milk. Beat well. Add the ground poppy seeds, mix to combine, and set aside.

In a small heatproof bowl, dissolve yeast in 1/2 cup of warm milk. In the bowl of a stand mixer or large bowl, combine flour, 3/4 cup sugar, salt, and eggs. Add the remaining 1 1/2 cups of warm milk, 4 ounces butter, and the yeast mixture. Beat with the paddle attachment, or by hand, until smooth. The dough will be sticky at this point.

Scrape the dough into a clean, greased bowl. Sprinkle the top with a little flour and cover. Leave in a warm place for 50 minutes or until doubled in size. Punch the dough down and turn it out on a floured surface. Divide the dough in half and shape each half into a rectangle.

Divide half of the filling over one rectangle of dough and the other half over the other rectangle. Roll up each rectangle like a jelly roll. Turn the ends under so the filling doesn't leak out. Transfer the rolls to a parchment-lined or greased pan, cover and allow to rise again until doubled in size.

Heat the oven to 350 F. Brush the top of the rolls with extra melted butter. Bake for 50 to 65 minutes or until the buns are golden brown. Remove the buns from the oven and let cool. Dust rolls with powdered sugar and cut the buns into half-inch slices.

Pineapple Crumble Cake

Preparation time: 20 minutes
Cooking time: 55 minutes
Nutrition facts (per serving): 321 Calories (Fat 21g, Protein 46g, Fiber 12g)

Ingredients (8 servings)
1 1/4 cups all-purpose flour
1/3 cup of sugar
3 tablespoons packed light or dark brown sugar
4 ounces (1 stick) cold butter, cut into pieces
4 ounces (1 stick) of softened butter
2/3 cup sugar
1 large egg at room temperature
2 large egg yolks at room temperature.
1 1/2 teaspoons vanilla
3 tablespoons of sour cream at room temperature
1 1/4 cups all-purpose flour
1 teaspoon of baking powder
1/4 teaspoon of salt
1 medium fresh pineapple or 20 ounces of pre-cut fresh pineapple

Preparation
For peeling a whole pineapple, cut the crown and the bottom of. Stand the pineapple upright and remove the tough skin around with a sharp chef's knife and a sawing movement. Cut the pineapple in half vertically and remove the core from both halves. Cut the halves into 1/2 inch thick half rings. Cover with plastic and reserve.

Prepare the crumb topping by mixing flour and 1/3 cup sugar and 3 tablespoons brown sugar in a large bowl. Cut the butter into the mixture as you would for pie dough until large crumbs form. Transfer the crumbs to another bowl and reserve.

Place the rack in the center of the oven and heat to 360 F. Spray a 9-inch square pan with cooking spray. In the same large bowl in which you made the crumbs, prepare the cake batter by whisking 4 ounces of butter and 2/3 cup sugar with an electric mixer until fluffy. Add the whole egg and yolks one at a time, beating after each addition. Add vanilla and beat on medium speed for 40 seconds. Add the sour cream and blend into a mixture. The batter will look curdled. In a separate bowl, combine 1 1/4 cups of flour, baking powder and salt. Add the flour mixture to the batter and beat on low speed for 30 seconds, then on medium for 1 minute or until thick and creamy.

Pour the batter into the prepared pan. Arrange the pineapple half-rings to cover the surface of the cake evenly. Sprinkle evenly with crumb topping. Place the pan on a baking sheet and bake for 53 to 58 minutes or until a toothpick inserted in the center of the cake comes out clean. Let the cake cool in the pan for 40 minutes, cut into squares, and serve warm or at room temperature.

Polish Angel Wings (Chruściki)

Preparation time: 15 minutes
Cooking time: 10 minutes
Nutrition Facts (per serving): 166 Calories (Fat 4 g, Carbohydrates 4 g, Protein 3 g)

Ingredients (24 servings)
5 egg yolks
1 egg
1/2 teaspoon of salt
1/4 cup confectioner's sugar
1/4 cup cream
1 teaspoon of vanilla extract
1 tablespoon of rum or brandy
2 cups of flour
1-liter canola or vegetable oil
Confectioners' sugar

Preparation
Combine egg yolks, whole egg, and salt in the bowl of a mixer. Beat on high speed for 6 minutes or until thick and lemon-colored. Beat in confectioners' sugar, cream, vanilla, and rum. Add flour and beat for about 6 minutes until blisters appear in the dough. Transfer the dough to a floured plate, divide it in half, cover with plastic wrap, and let rest for at least 22 minutes.

Work with half the dough at a time and roll it out to 1/8 inch thickness. Cut into 2 inch wide strips. Cut these strips on the diagonal at 4-inch intervals. Heat 2 inches of oil in a large, deep skillet to medium-high heat. Make a slit in the center of each strip of dough. Pull one end through the slit to form an arc. Fry 6 wings at a time for 1 minute per side or until golden brown. Do not overcook; wings will bake quickly. Drain on paper towels. Sprinkle with confectioner's sugar or honey.

Polish Strawberry Kissel

Preparation time: 20 minutes
Cooking time: 10 minutes
Nutrition Facts (per serving): 100 Calories (Fat 1 g, Carbohydrates 23 g, Protein 1 g)

Ingredients (6 servings)

1 cup of water
1/2 cup sugar
3 tablespoons potato starch or 4 tablespoons cornstarch
1/2 cup of water
1 pound strawberries, peeled, washed, and crushed

Preparation

In a large saucepan, bring 1 cup of water and sugar to a boil and then remove from heat. Dissolve potato starch in 1/2 cup of cold water and stir it into the sugar-water mixture. Return to the heat and bring to boil, stirring constantly. Add strawberries and mix well. Divide into individual dessert bowls or one large bowl that has been rinsed with cold water. Refrigerate for 3 hours.

Polish Plum Pie
(Placek z Sliwkami)

Preparation time: 20 minutes
Cooking time: 40 minutes
Nutrition facts (per serving): 496 Calories (Fat 16g, Carbs 87g, Protein 8g)

Ingredients (12 servings)
Cake
2 1/3 cups all-purpose flour
2 1/2 teaspoons baking powder
3/4 teaspoon of salt
3/4 cup sugar
4 ounces butter
3/4 cup of milk
2 eggs
10 medium fresh plums

Streusel Topping
1/4 cup sugar
1/4 teaspoon of cloves
3 tablespoons butter, cold, cut into pieces

Preparation
Preheat oven to 355 F. Lightly brushes a 13 x 9-inch baking dish with cooking spray. In a large bowl, combine the flour, baking powder, salt, and 3/4 cup of sugar. Add eggs, butter and milk. Beat with a hand mixer on medium speed for 5 minutes or until all ingredients are combined. Pour the batter into the prepared pan. Place the plum halves on top, cut side up, and push them slightly down into the batter.

Chop the remaining 1/4 cup of sugar and cloves into 3 tablespoons of cold butter until crumbs form. Sprinkle it over the plums. Bake the cake on the middle oven rack for about 41-43 minutes or until a toothpick inserted in several places comes out clean.

Let the cake cool in the pan to absorb the juice from the plums, resulting in a particularly moist cake with an intense plum flavor. Sprinkle the top with confectioner's sugar, if desired, and cut the cake into 10-14 squares.

Polish Dried Fruit Compote

Preparation time: 5 minutes
Cooking time: 20 minutes
Nutrition Facts (per serving): 68 Calories (Fat 0 g, Protein 0 g, Carbohydrates 18g)

Ingredients (12 servings)
1 1/2 pounds of dried fruit (plums, apricots, figs, apples, peaches, pears, berries)
8 cups of water
8 whole cloves
2 cinnamon sticks
Lemon zest
1 cup sugar or to taste

Preparation
In a saucepan, add 8 cups of water, 1 1/2 pounds of your choice of dried fruit, 8 whole cloves, 2 cinnamon sticks, and, if using, lemon zest and sugar. Bring to the boil while stirring.

Reduce heat and simmer, covered, for about 22 minutes or until fruit is tender and the syrup has thickened slightly. Add more water if you prefer a more liquid consistency or, for a thicker compote, keep simmering to further reduce the moisture. Serve.

Apple Pancakes With Yeast

Preparation time: 20 minutes
Cooking time: 30 minutes
Nutrition Facts (per serving): 497 Calories (Fat 20 g, Carbohydrates 72g, Protein 9g)

Ingredients (12 servings)
1 2/3 ounces fresh yeast
¼ ounces sugar
2 ounces of water
3 eggs
½ ounces vanilla sugar
5 ounces sugar
17 ounces milk
25 ounces all-purpose flour
A pinch of salt
1 pound apples
1/2 cup vegetable oil (or if needed, for frying)
1 pound apples
17 ounces apple juice
1 ounces sugar
1 teaspoon cinnamon

Preparation
Mix the yeast with ¼ ounce sugar and let rise in a warm place. Beat the eggs with vanilla sugar and 5 ounces sugar. Gradually add milk, flour, a pinch of salt, and the leavened yeast. Mix all ingredients well with a wooden spoon and work the batter until air bubbles appear.

Wash and peel 1 pound apples and remove the seeds. Slice them and immerse them in the batter and set aside in a warm place. Heat the oil in a large frying pan and with a spoon, add the batter with the apple slices in the form of small pancakes. Fry them over low heat, turning them now and then to make sure they don't brown too much.

Wash and peel 1 pound of apples, remove the seeds and cut into slices. Pour the apple juice into a saucepan, add the apple slices, along with 1 ounce sugar and cinnamon, and cook until the apples are soft. Put this in a mixer and blend until smooth. Serve the sauce with the pancakes.

Faworki

Preparation time: 20 minutes
Cooking time: 2 minutes
Nutrition facts (per serving): 126 Calories (Protein 2.5 g, carbohydrates 16.6g, Cholesterol 65.5mg)

Ingredients (20 servings)
2 ½ cups all-purpose flour
2 tablespoons butter, softened
1 tablespoon rum
1 pinch of salt
2 cups vegetable oil for frying
6 large egg yolks
3 tablespoons sour cream
2 tablespoons white sugar
½ cup confectioner's sugar, to taste

Preparation
Combine rum, sour cream, flour, egg yolks, sugar, butter, and salt in a large bowl. Mix into a dough. Knead the dough lightly and roll it out on a floured work surface. Cut into strips 3 inch long and 1 inch wide. Cut a slit in the center of each strip. Twist and pull one end through the slot. Heat oil in a deep-fryer or large pan. Test the temperature by dropping a dough twist in it. The oil is ready when it turns brown and floats to the surface. Bake the dough in batches for one minute per side or until golden brown. Drain on a plate lined with kitchen paper. Sprinkle with confectioner's sugar.

Holiday Crescent Cookies

Preparation time: 30 minutes
Cooking time: 15 minutes
Nutrition Facts (per serving): 100 Calories (Fat 27 g, Protein 18 g, Carbohydrates 14g)

Ingredients (55 servings)

3 cups flour
1/2 pound cold butter cut into cubes
6 egg yolks
1/2 cup sour cream
6 proteins
1/2 pound powdered sugar
3 cups walnuts finely chopped

Preparation

In a bowl, using a pastry blender or fork, mix the butter into the flour, creating a coarse, crumb-like consistency. Mix the egg yolks and sour cream in a separate bowl. Add to the flour mixture. Mix and knead lightly until the mixture is similar to pie dough. Form small balls the size of a walnut and refrigerate overnight (about 55 balls). Place the egg whites in an airtight container and refrigerate. The next day beat the egg whites until stiff. Add icing sugar and beat well. Stir in the nuts and refrigerate.

Polish Cheesecake

Preparation time: 45 minutes
Cooking time: 60 minutes
Nutrition facts (per serving): 709 Calories (Fat 47g, Protein 24g, Carbs 50g)

Ingredients (12 servings)

9 ounces butter

3 pound full or semi-fat cottage cheese, minced at least twice

10 eggs, egg whites, and yolks separated

1 pound brown sugar

6 tablespoons semolina

1 ½ ounces custard powder

Seeds from 2 vanilla pods

1 teaspoon vanilla extract

1 cup of double cream (30% fat)

3/4 cup of your favorite dried fruit (raisins or candied orange zest)

Preparation

Beat the butter until light and fluffy. Slowly add the cottage cheese, still beating, until fully incorporated. In a separate bowl, beat the egg yolks with the sugar until creamy and white. Add to the cheesecake mixture and mix to combine. Add semolina, custard powder, vanilla and mix until just combined. Beat the whipped cream in a bowl until it forms soft peaks. Beat the egg whites in another bowl, also to soft peaks. Gently stir the cream, egg whites, and dried fruit into the cheesecake mixture. Grease a baking pan and line it with parchment paper. Place the cheesecake mixture in a baking pan and smooth. Bake for about 65 minutes at 340 F. Cool and refrigerate overnight.

Polish Apple Pie (Szarlotka)

Preparation time: 1 hour
Cooking time: 1 hour
Nutrition Facts: 270 Calories (Fat 9g, Protein 4g, Cholesterol 75mg)

Ingredients (8 servings)
Crust
4 cups unbleached all-purpose flour
½ cup of sugar
2 teaspoons baking powder
1 cup (1/2 pounds) salted butter, softened
4 eggs
1 teaspoon pure vanilla extract
3 tablespoons milk

Filling
2 pounds firm baking apple (Gala or Pink Lady), peeled, cored and sliced
2 pounds soft baking apple (Red Delicious, Braeburn, or Fuji), peeled, cored, and sliced
2 teaspoons of cinnamon

Preparation
Crust
Preheat the oven to 355 F. In a large bowl, combine the flour, sugar, and baking powder. Slice in the butter, using a pastry blender or fork until the mixture resembles coarse crumbs. Stir in the eggs and vanilla extract until the mixture is smooth. Add the milk, 1 tablespoon at a time, and mix with your hands after each addition until a firm but slightly sticky dough forms. Add extra milk if necessary.

Turn the dough on the counter and knead it quickly a few times to bring the dough together. Divide the dough into two pieces, about 2/3 and 1/3 of the dough. Wrap the smaller portion in plastic wrap and place in the freezer for 40 minutes. Press the larger part into a greased 9-inch springform pan. Bake the bottom crust in the preheated oven for 16 minutes or until puffy and starting to turn golden on the edges. When the crust is cooked, remove it from the oven to a cooling rack.

Filling

While the bottom crust is baking, mix the apples and cinnamon in a large sauté pan or large saucepan. Heat the apples over low heat and cook for 6-8 minutes or until the apples soften and the mixture turns fragrant. Remove the mixture from the heat.

Put everything together. Divide the warm filling over the warm crust. Remove the last 1/3 of the crust from the freezer and grate it over the apple filling with a cheese grater or crumble it over the apples with your fingers. Place an aluminum foil-lined baking sheet in the oven on the wire rack below where the pie is going to catch the dripping from the springform pan. Return the pie to the oven and bake for 42-46 minutes, until the top is golden brown. Remove the pie from the oven and let it cool completely before serving.

For any $2,99 you can buy other cookbooks with 111 recipes from Italy, Greece, Iran, Armenia, Russia, Romania, Turkey, Syria, Spain and many more…

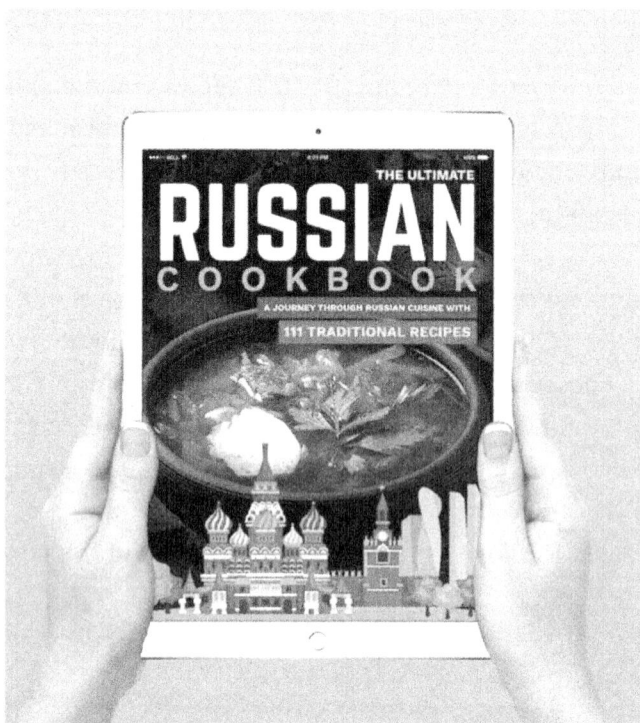

Available at Amazon, the full list is available at

If you liked Polish food, discover to how cook DELICIOUS recipes from neighboring Balkan countries!

Within these pages, you'll learn 35 authentic recipes from a Balkan cook. These aren't ordinary recipes you'd find on the Internet, but recipes that were closely guarded by our Balkan mothers and passed down from generation to generation.

Main Dishes, Appetizers, and Desserts included!

If you want to learn how to make Croatian green peas stew, and 32 other authentic Balkan recipes, then start with our book!

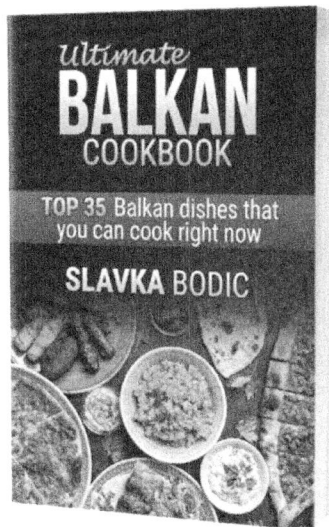

If you're a Mediterranean dieter who wants to know the secrets of the Mediterranean diet, dieting, and cooking, then you're about to discover how to master cooking meals on a Mediterranean diet right now!

In fact, if you want to know how to make Mediterranean food, then this new e-book - "The 30-minute Mediterranean diet" - gives you the answers to many important questions and challenges every Mediterranean dieter faces, including:

- How can I succeed with a Mediterranean diet?
- What kind of recipes can I make?
- What are the key principles to this type of diet?
- What are the suggested weekly menus for this diet?
- Are there any cheat items I can make?

... and more!

If you're serious about cooking meals on a Mediterranean diet and you really want to know how to make Mediterranean food, then you need to grab a copy of "The 30-minute Mediterranean diet" right now.

Prepare 111 recipes with several ingredients in less than 30 minutes!

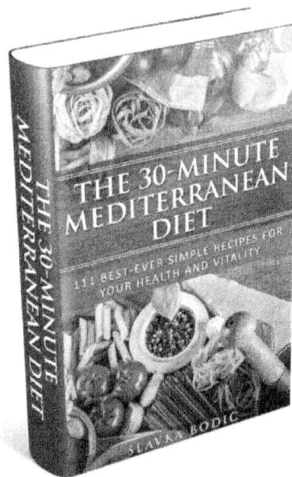

Order **HERE** now for only **$2,99!**

What could be better than a home-cooked meal? Maybe only a Greek homemade meal.

Do not get discouraged if you have no Greek roots or friends. Now you can make a Greek food feast in your kitchen.

This ultimate Greek cookbook offers you 111 best dishes of this cuisine! From more famous gyros to more exotic Kota Kapama this cookbook keeps it easy and affordable.

All the ingredients necessary are wholesome and widely accessible. The author's picks are as flavorful as they are healthy. The dishes described in this cookbook are "what Greek mothers have made for decades."

Full of well-balanced and nutritious meals, this handy cookbook includes many vegan options. Discover a plethora of benefits of Mediterranean cuisine, and you may fall in love with cooking at home.

Inspired by a real food lover, this collection of delicious recipes will taste buds utterly satisfied.

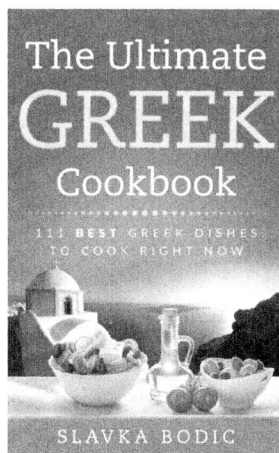

The Ultimate
GREEK
Cookbook
111 BEST GREEK DISHES
TO COOK RIGHT NOW

SLAVKA BODIC

Order **HERE** now for only **$2,99!**

Maybe to try exotic Serbian cuisine?

From succulent sarma, soups, warm and cold salads to delectable desserts, the plethora of flavors will satisfy the most jaded foodie. Have a taste of a new culture with this **traditional Serbian cookbook.**

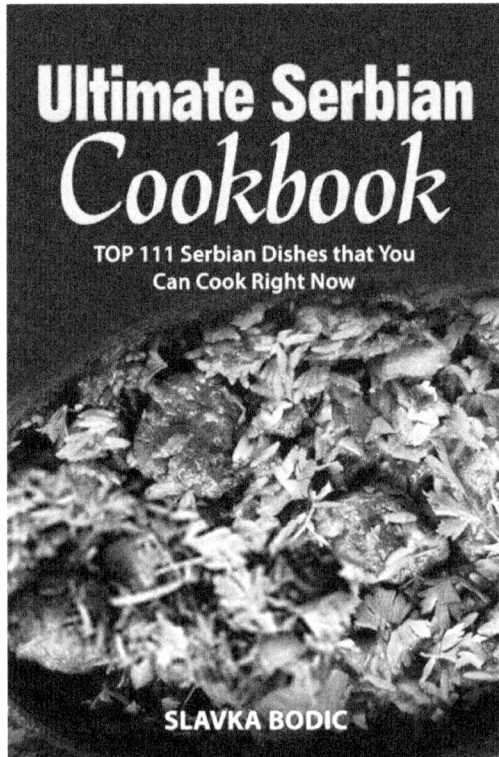

ONE LAST THING

If you enjoyed this book or found it useful, I'd be very grateful if you could find the time to post a short review on Amazon. Your support really does make a difference and I read all the reviews personally, so I can get your feedback and make this book even better.

Thanks again for your support!

Please send me your feedback at

www.balkanfood.org

Printed in Great Britain
by Amazon